SERVE WITH HONOR

SERVE
WITH
HONOR

HELPS FOR MISSIONARIES

RANDY L. BOTT

Deseret Book Company
Salt Lake City, Utah

Library of Congress Cataloging-in-Publication Data

Bott, Randy L., 1945–
    Serve with honor : helps for missionaries / Randy L. Bott.
      p.   cm.
    Includes bibliographical references and index.
    ISBN 0-87579-955-8 (pbk.)
    1. Church of Jesus Christ of Latter-day Saints—Missions—Handbooks, manuals, etc. 2. Mormon Church—Missions—Handbooks, manuals, etc. 3. Missionaries—Handbooks, manuals, etc. 4. Youth—Religious life—Handbooks, manuals, etc. I. Title.

BX8661.B684   1995
266'.9332—dc20   95-35438
                                                      CIP

Printed in the United States of America   7973-2994
Bang Printing, Brainerd, MN

10 9   8

To my wife, Vickie, who exemplifies,
more than anyone I know,
what it means to serve with honor

To our daughters Jennie and Jami
and the countless students
who have shared with me
their missionary experiences

And to the six hundred young men and women
with whom we had the privilege of serving in Fresno,
who learned by experience
the joy of serving with honor

CONTENTS

CONTENTS

INTRODUCTION

MANY WONDERFUL BOOKS HAVE been written about missionary work. Some focus on the scriptures; others contain
advice from modern-day prophets. Both sources are necessary and informative. This book is the result of nearly a lifetime of involvement in missionary-related activities: serving
as a full-time missionary, teaching young people who are
preparing to serve missions, and serving as a mission president. In this book I have quoted lightly from the scriptures
and the teachings of modern-day prophets. I have taken a
rather broad approach. My hope is to offer practical, down-
to-earth advice on matters essential to serving a successful
mission.

I have tried diligently not only to identify different
aspects of mission life that pose the greatest challenges but
also to offer suggestions to help missionaries cope with these
difficulties. This book is not a comprehensive handbook
designed to cover all situations that you might encounter on
your mission. Rather, it gives examples of circumstances generally found in all missions. The advice in this book is strictly
my own; if any of it contradicts rules set down by your mission president, follow his counsel.

This book will not attempt to reiterate what is contained
in officially printed Church materials. Topics like how to find

investigators, friendship, teach, baptize, and fellowship are masterfully covered in the *Missionary Guide* (Salt Lake City: The Church of Jesus Christ of Latter-day Saints, 1988). Techniques used effectively in your particular mission will be taught at zone conferences and in other mission training sessions. The gospel study guide you will receive at the Missionary Training Center (often called the MTC) will provide an excellent curriculum for broadening your understanding of gospel doctrine and the scriptures.

My intent in writing is to help make your transition into missionary life as painless and enjoyable as possible by identifying potential challenges. Being forewarned, missionaries can avoid the surprise factor—facing a new, possibly unnerving situation for which you may not be adequately prepared—a circumstance that, if it discourages you unduly, can be turned into one of the adversary's most effective weapons. Not every situation will apply to every mission. Not every missionary will face every problem. If reading this book helps you in any way to be a more effective missionary, then my purpose in writing has been served. A mission is neither the greatest time of your life nor the worst time. It all depends on how you serve. This book will not make you a good missionary any more than wearing a suit will make you an honorable priesthood bearer or wearing a dress and name tag will make you a diligent sister. The choice is yours. At this time in your life you have only one mission to serve, so do it up right. *Serve with honor.*

2

···········

THE DAY YOU ARRIVE

THE FIRST DAY! A BLUR, A HEADACHE, a time of possible anxiety but certain excitement, a time to make history. You will have only one first day in your mission area. This day will be the first of many other firsts. You spend your first night in your mission area. You meet your first mission president. You meet your first companion. You eat your first meal of your actual mission. You are assigned to your first area of labor. You may teach your first discussion. You may commit your first investigator to baptism. You may perform your first priesthood ordinance. The list of firsts is endless.

It makes but little difference *what* happens to you. It makes all the difference in the world *how* you react to what happens. Everything happens so fast. At the airport you may get a headache from the normal anxieties and pressures associated with saying good-bye to your family and friends, and getting your bags checked through to the correct destination. Don't be surprised. Because of the anticipation of leaving the MTC, you may not have slept much the night before. Fatigue is common among newly arriving missionaries. Unfortunately, you probably won't have much time to rest when you first arrive at the mission home. If your mission president holds an orientation meeting, you may find it difficult to concentrate because of your fatigue. But even though the president is very excited to have you there, he surely is mindful of how physically taxing the trip has been for you.

At the orientation meeting, the president may ask if you have any questions. Don't be embarrassed if the answer is no. You haven't had enough experience to know what to ask! As time passes, you will have questions. Don't be afraid to ask them. The sooner you can develop confidence in the president, the easier it will be to allow him to help you adjust. Some missionaries, not really believing or understanding that one man can know and be interested in so many missionaries, remain somewhat aloof from the mission president. A special endowment comes with the office, enabling each president to meet the needs of those missionaries who serve with him. That is just one of the miracles of being a mission president. Trust him.

From the day of your arrival, keep a record of your mission. Many feelings you experience will prompt thoughts and ideas that will be lost forever unless you record them. If you start this habit early in your mission, it will be easy to keep writing. But if you start out on the wrong foot, it can be very difficult to correct your course later. According to your president's direction, you should immediately write a letter home informing your parents of your new address and letting them know you have arrived safely. Express your love for your family; it will begin a process that will result in great blessings or even miracles for them.

Although you may be so keyed up that you can hardly sleep, try to get a good night's sleep that first night. If there is anything more exciting and challenging than the first day, it is the second day. Every new thing you can imagine, plus many unexpected things, will happen to you on the second day. And you will only live one second day—so take full advantage of it. Don't panic. If you miss a bus or forget to get off in the right place, it may cause some concern (especially if you don't speak or understand the language!), but it will not result in death. Learn to laugh at yourself when you make honest mistakes! You may feel like you are in total control of the situation, but after a few months into your mission, you will realize you were a total space case. You may laugh at how "in charge" you thought you were.

Don't trust your memory. Write on a piece of paper your trainer's name, address, and phone number. Even if you become temporarily lost, you can usually show the note to a native and receive some help. If you miss a connection, a phone call to the president and to your companion will put a lot of worried minds at ease. When an elder or sister is missing, a 2:00 A.M. phone call is much more relaxing than anxiety producing. Almost everybody is willing to help when they know you are in trouble. You will make many good friends for yourself and for the Church when you allow others to exercise their Christianity by helping you.

Don't make any judgments based on the first few weeks. Missionaries who decide after a few weeks that the mission just isn't for them make a terrible mistake. Naturally, almost any new environment will seem foreign to you. The urge is to run. The wise missionary realizes that these feelings are normal and doesn't take them too seriously. If you experience feelings of not belonging and these feelings last for more than a week or two, call the mission president. This doesn't necessarily mean something is wrong with you; it might just mean you haven't learned how to relax and adjust. You will learn important lessons as you serve, and they will greatly benefit you in the future.

Sometimes, when trying to fit in, you may be tempted to

be a bit silly. It is difficult to know exactly how to act when you suddenly find yourself in a new environment and are getting acquainted with new friends. Remember, all the missionaries you meet in those first few days have experienced what you are going through and know exactly how you feel. They survived, and so will you. If you are going to make a mistake in the way you act, err on the side of being too conservative. Try being a little more quiet than normal. Stand back and watch how things operate. Don't try on the first day to fix everything you see wrong. Chances are, there are reasons why things are done the way they are. If not, you will have plenty of time later to suggest changes.

As quickly as your head stops spinning and your feet are on the ground, find out what is expected of you. Each mission will have a training program that will walk you through those requirements step by step. Some requirements may seem a little strange. Until you have had a chance to see the rationale behind the rules, follow them; learn the "why" later. You may be overwhelmed by how much memorization, reading, and studying are required. If you try to tackle the entire process at once, you will surely become frustrated. If you sit down with your trainer and break the requirements down into manageable pieces, you will do fine. The first and normal reaction is to want to throw both hands in the air and quit. Thankfully, very few missionaries actually do that. Probably a quiet laughing session will help reduce the stress level. As you learn to turn to your Heavenly Father, you will begin to develop a nurturing relationship that will enable you to tackle large assignments in the future and will make your present problems seem like child's play.

Don't make any snap judgments about the missionaries you live or serve with. They may not know quite how to act toward you either. Give them the benefit of the doubt. If they make some social mistakes, forgive them. If they are not very sensitive to your needs, kindly inform them. If you get the impression that they are trying to take advantage of your newness, let them know what you perceive; usually they are not trying to bully you or give you a hard time. There should never be any initiation or hazing in the mission. If there is, inform the mission president immediately. Sometimes, innocent games become cruel experiences if they are not stopped.

From the first moment, establish a habit of sincere prayer—a good way to put life into an eternal perspective. When no one else around understands how you are feeling, the Lord does understand. He has descended below all things, so he knows exactly how to help you through the rough spots. He is always there and has promised he will not leave you alone and comfortless. If you can establish or improve your personal relationship with the Lord from the very first day of your mission, your feelings of loneliness will be scarce. Be positive, focused, and motivated from the day you enter the mission field until the day you leave. That will establish a pattern that will help you become a good missionary and will bless you for the rest of your life.

3

BEING A GREENY

WHEN YOU ARRIVE IN YOUR mission area, you will be one of the least experienced missionaries in the entire world! That sounds pretty scary until you realize that several hundred of you left the MTC on the same day. No matter what the term is in your mission (according to the language you speak), the meaning is the same: You are a "greeny!"

I remember a wise General Authority who many years ago recounted his experience of when he was first called as a General Authority. He felt that his abilities paled in comparison to the wisdom and confidence of the other Brethren. He sought the counsel of his father, a wise sheepherder. After explaining his fears, he waited for his father's reply. This father offered his General Authority son timely advice that has in turn helped me a great deal: "Son, just graze around the edges for a while!"

Very often, young missionaries from the MTC think they know more about running a mission than the mission president does. They almost always think they know more about being an assistant to the president, a zone leader, or a district leader than elders who are called to those offices. Not infrequently, new missionaries may know more about missionary work than their trainers. My advice is the same as that of the General Authority's father: "Graze around the edges for a while." Don't try to quickly right every wrong you think you see, because there may be reasons why things are done a certain way. Weighty decisions are easy to make when you are not burdened with the facts!

Don't take this counsel too personally. You are a valuable person, and your opinion does count. The counsel to withhold judgment will help you see things in perspective. Perhaps you do have better ideas than your trainer or your leaders, but until you have established yourself as a credible missionary, nobody will take you seriously. You must learn to be a good follower before you can be a good leader.

As a greeny, you will be given a grace period. During this time, your trainer will carry the burden of planning the day, leading the teaching of investigators, orchestrating your training, and providing you with opportunities to learn and grow. The extra time created by your trainer's willingness to help you should be used to learn the language, master the discussions, study the gospel, and familiarize yourself with the mission routine.

As soon as you are ready (usually before you think), the trainer will start to shift more of the load onto your shoulders. Your first reaction will probably be to complain that you are not quite ready. Be brave and accept responsibility. If you seem to fail, maintain a keen sense of humor.

Those who are learning languages will have ample opportunity to laugh at themselves. While you were growing up, it probably was not "cool" to be laughed at. Most people who speak a foreign language laugh at you because they are amused by your willingness to try a new and difficult language. Most people you serve would like to be like you but don't have the courage to try. Before long, they will stand in awe as you teach a lesson or talk in church or perform a sacred, saving ordinance. Enjoy your time as a greeny.

If you are uncomfortable with not knowing everything, you're not alone. Even your trainer won't know all the answers. If you ask good questions, you can cut your training time by more than half. Unfortunately, your trainer may have forgotten how it was to be brand-new; he may take for granted that you know how to work the daily planner, how to make dinner appointments, or how to read the scriptures and learn from them. Your constant questioning will remind him how much you do or don't know. If your questions irritate him, ask him how he expects you to learn these things. You might even suggest that if he anticipates your needs and volunteers his insights, you won't need to ask so many questions.

Your goal should be to experience all the trials you will face when *you* become a senior companion. If you shy away from new and bigger tasks, you only postpone the time when you will be able to take over an area and train a junior companion. Your own creative strategies of doing missionary work will remain largely dormant while you are a junior companion.

If you are going to make mistakes in technique, make them in your first area, because after you leave your first area, people will assume you are a seasoned missionary. Mistakes you were reluctant to correct in your training area will haunt you in your second area.

If your trainer is disobedient or lazy, you must have a plan of action firmly in mind. Decide on the first day how you want to serve. Don't feel discouraged or believe you are the only diligent missionary in the field. That obviously is not the case. If your trainer does not hold regular companionship study sessions with you, encourage him to start. If he refuses, study on your own during that time. It is not "narking" or tattling to tell the mission president in an interview that the training is not going as planned. You deserve a strong start; if you don't get it, you have the right to at least ask for help on how to compensate for your trainer's failure. Don't be quick to ask for another trainer, though—your next companion may be even more casual. You will want to learn to get along with and motivate all kinds of companions during your mission, and you may as well start with your trainer.

Do not follow your trainer in breaking mission rules. Establish on your first day in the field that you plan to obey all the rules given in the *Missionary Handbook* (the little white rule book that missionaries carry) and by the mission president. Let your trainer know from the beginning that you expect him to give you the kind of start that he wished he had received. In the very unlikely event that your trainer is grossly disobedient, don't hesitate to call the president for advice. Remember, if he leaves you and gets into trouble that could threaten his membership, his worthiness to continue his mission may be questioned. Save him from himself if necessary.

More likely, your trainer will become your best friend. As he works with you, trust him. Do as he directs as long as it's within mission rules. Be willing to consider his suggested changes and improvements. You will not yet have discovered the best teaching techniques and skills, so learn from your trainer and make the most of your time as a greeny.

4

YOUR RELATIONSHIP TO THE MISSION PRESIDENT

WHO IS YOUR BEST MORTAL friend during your mission? Your answer should be "the mission president." Because the adversary works to divide and conquer, some unfortunate missionaries do not understand the true relationship that should exist between them and their president. The mission president is not perfect. But if you learn to trust him, he will become one of your lifelong heroes. He has been given the spiritual keys necessary to guide you through this exciting time of life. He will differ from the mission presidents where your father, mother, brothers, or sisters may have served. He may be tall, short, fat, or skinny, but appearances will not matter. The sooner you learn to trust him, the quicker he will be able to identify your personal needs. His real spiritual insight comes as he interacts with you. How can he get to know so many missionaries? Are you just a number to him? Does he really care about you individually? These questions and many more deserve answers.

How does he get to know you? In zone conferences, in interviews, at socials, through phone calls, through your weekly letter to the president, and through prayer. As you sit in a zone conference with so many other missionaries, you might wonder how the mission president could possibly get to know you. It really isn't difficult. As the president looks at missionaries' faces, those who are doing well and keeping the rules have a certain aura of peace, unlike disobedient missionaries.

For those of you who wonder whether you are judged according to whom you associate with, the answer is yes. Since "likes" attract in the gospel, you will naturally gravitate toward those who have similar interests and the same attitudes toward leadership, the gospel, and life. If you do not want to be labeled as one of the "back-row crew," don't sit on the back row. If you do sit there, don't be surprised if you gain the reputation of being too casual. If you are concerned about missionaries talking behind your back about your lack of devotion, watch carefully whom you associate with on preparation day (the day known as "P day," most of which is set aside for missionaries to attend to personal matters such as letter writing, shopping, and enjoying wholesome recreational and cultural activities) and in district and zone activities. Are you developing a casual attitude toward the divine charge to serve with all your heart?

When the mission president shakes hands with you before or after the zone conference, look him in the eye. Too many missionaries look guilty because they refuse to meet the president eye to eye. That doesn't mean you have to stare at him or his wife. It does mean that if you consciously look down or away every time your eyes meet, you send a strong message that all may not be well in your personal life.

Because the mission president has between one hundred fifty and two hundred missionaries to supervise, use wisely your precious interview time with him. When he asks how you are doing, don't say "fine" if you are not; be honest and direct. As a way to get straight to the point, my first interview question was "How are you doing?" The second question was always "How are you really doing?" In other words: "Don't put me on. We don't have all day, and I'm only here to help. Trust me and tell me what's on your mind."

The normal interview cycle (unless you serve in a geographically huge mission) is from four to six weeks. The interview may take place before or after the zone conference or at a separate time. Whenever it is held, be sensitive to the time restraints of the mission president and also to other missionaries waiting to be interviewed or waiting to take you home. If you need extra time, ask if you can set a time for another interview. Don't be offended if the mission president suggests another time; he wants to give you the time you need, but he doesn't want to detain others who have schedules to meet. Be sensitive to other missionaries' needs. Practice a little empathy—put yourself in the president's place—and you will generally see why he does what he does.

In the interview, describe as concisely as possible any problems or concern-producing situations. Don't try to give every little detail. Some missionaries take so long describing a problem that little time remains for investigating solutions. Don't expect the president to answer all your questions or tell you how to solve all your problems. The mission is meant to be a place of learning for you. If the president were to solve all your problems, you would never learn to find solutions through study and prayer. Take his suggestions and try to implement them, but don't expect an immediate answer or solution. Many times the directions or insight I received came later while I was driving, retiring for the night, or waking from a deep sleep. The Lord works on his own timetable, even where mission presidents are concerned.

Be careful not to confess your companion's sins. It is a real temptation to blame everything on your companion. You can always describe a situation without assessing fault. You may also believe that you are the only missionary struggling to keep up with missionary requirements. That isn't true. Everyone struggles in one or more areas. An honest difference of opinion between you and your companion does not spell doom or failure. The mission president will have had much broader experience in life and in the mission than you. Usually he will be able to tell you whether your experiences are normal or whether you should be concerned.

Ask for special interviews very sparingly. At district, zone, and half-mission activities, make it a point to chat with the president. He will probably be more relaxed than usual and able to deal with problems that otherwise would have to take a back burner. At the activities, be sensitive to the other missionaries who also would like a little one-on-one time with the president. You may discover that you become irritated when some elder or sister monopolizes the president's time. If you have a pressing need, contact the president for a special time when you might be able to meet.

Some missionaries hold back through lack of familiarity, fear, or a desire not to want to burden the president. You can overcome the feeling of unfamiliarity by initiating contact. Most mission presidents welcome the opportunity to chat with missionaries. If you fear the president, it is probably because you don't know him or do not understand why he is there. Your success is his success; your failure is his failure. Let him help smooth the rough spots and create an environment where you will most likely succeed. Missionaries not wanting to burden the president cost me more sleepless nights, more gray hairs, and more anxiety than almost anything else. If you ignore a problem, it will probably not go away. In fact, if you stuff all your problems under the rug, they begin to accumulate (with interest!) until they finally blow up. Then, instead of a bandage, you need major surgery to correct the problem. What did you save by not being open and frank with the president? Nothing! Silence costs so much that you will regret being so shortsighted in your quest to help the mission run smoothly.

Another disease you can help destroy is the habit of criticizing the president. Your president will be human—I don't know of any that aren't. He will make mistakes, but they will not always be the ones the missionaries think he is making. Usually he will err in trying to be too kind or to do too much for you. He gains nothing from your distress or failing; happy missionaries make happy mission presidents. If you hear anyone criticize your president, let them know you disagree. Almost always the criticism is made because the person criticizing doesn't have access to enough information to make a wise judgment. If the gossip is particularly vicious or potentially damaging, call the president and inform him of what is being said. Don't let the adversary blindside your leader. When he hurts, you all hurt. When he prospers, life is great for you too. Most of the time, it will not be necessary to bring petty criticism to his attention. He will almost always be aware of the problem before you mention it. The fact that you care enough to protect him raises your value to him.

Your president has been blessed with keys to administer the mission under the direction of the General Authorities. Just as you, as a missionary, receive blessings and abilities because of your sacred calling, so too is the mission president magnified by the Lord for his willingness to sacrifice in your behalf.

Finally, when you return home, you will want to keep an occasional correspondence with your president. He will be a special person in your life until one of you passes away. His interest will always be in helping further your success. Remember that with over six hundred missionaries who served with him, he may not be able to correspond with you as frequently as he would like, because of the continuing demands on his time.

5

....

YOUR TRAINER

EITHER THE DAY YOU ARRIVE in the mission field or the next day, you will be assigned to work with the most important person (to that point) in your mission—your trainer. His or her size, color, appearance, and time in the mission will be of little significance. Your ideals and expectations of mission life will result largely from the teachings of your trainer.

Your trainer must take you from your present state and mold you into a polished missionary. That will require change on your part. In spite of the enthusiasm you brought from the MTC, you definitely lack experience. You are not in the mission to compete with your trainer or anyone else, but are to work together to master as quickly as possible those skills that will make you an effective missionary. Learn to work as companions rather than as two individuals.

The mission president has tried to find the right person to train you. Your trainer may not be what you expected, but trust that your Heavenly Father really does know and love you. He will inspire the president to put you with someone who will provide the training and experiences that will help prepare you to fulfill callings you will have on your mission and later in your life. You can learn from negative experiences as well as from positive ones. From my own experience, I did not always know why certain missionaries were put with certain trainers, but usually it became evident as time passed.

On the day you arrive to your first area, try to establish a good working relationship with your trainer, who will have been given instructions on how to train you. Usually a packet will be sent with you with forms to help guide your trainer through the training process. Training is not easy. It will require substantial sacrifice on the trainer's part to properly prepare you. He will have to give up personal study time and carry most of the load of proselyting for the first few weeks until you start to become effective.

If you have questions (and you'll probably have a bunch of them!), don't be afraid to ask them. The only stupid question is the one that is not asked. But before asking, see if you can figure out the answers on your own. It is frustrating to the trainer to be asked over and over questions that could be mastered if you would only concentrate a little more. If your trainer shows signs of irritation, check to see if you are being as attentive as you should be.

Learn how to deal with every phase of mission life. Some tricks of the trade will make the administrative requirements of a mission much easier. Something as simple as a monthly dinner calendar can eliminate trying to remember who signed up to feed you and when. It will help you avoid embarrassing mistakes and forgotten appointments. Keep your eyes open, and you will learn most of what you need to streamline your routine affairs.

Your trainer will be invaluable in helping you learn how to study the gospel on a regular, consistent basis. In seminary or church you may have learned how to cram for an assignment or a talk, but learning to organize your study time effectively is a real talent. Your trainer will have had much more experience than you in this area, but if your trainer isn't very good at it, check with other missionaries who seem to have mastered the skill. Make sure your trainer keeps you on a regular study schedule until the habit is so deeply ingrained that it becomes an unconscious, daily practice.

Companionship study will teach you many new skills. This may be the first time you and another person will talk seriously about Church doctrine, scripture, personality characteristics, and interpersonal skills. It may be awkward at first, but keep at it until it becomes something you look forward to every day. Because study requires effort and discipline, some choose to avoid it—a major mistake. This ability to plan and communicate will bless your marriage as you and your spouse discuss problems when you begin your own family.

It would be unusual if a trainer hesitated to hold companionship study, but should this happen, you have the right to insist it be held. If it doesn't happen, you should contact your leaders immediately. You can't afford to miss out on this valuable skill that will serve you faithfully for the rest of your life. You can make study easier by establishing a set time every morning. If you seem eager and willing, your trainer may be more enthusiastic about companionship study. Suggest ways that you think the companionship study sessions could be more effective. Let your trainer know how you learn best. It may take awhile before you know how you prefer to be taught.

Be creative in your approach. Some missionaries have a difficult time studying the *Missionary Guide* daily. A reward may provide the necessary motivation to study every day. When language study is part of your companionship study, make it a game to learn how to say things properly and to increase your vocabulary. When I trained one new missionary during my first mission, we discovered he was quite a master of the English language. He would give me an English word, and I would try to define it. In return I would give him a Samoan word that he would try to define. During one eight-mile walk between villages, I failed to correctly define one word he gave me in English, and he never got one of my words in Samoan. Before we finished our time together, I had greatly benefitted from his English skills, and he had become a more polished speaker of Samoan. We relished those sessions when we could challenge each other not only in language but also in matters of doctrine, scripture, customs, and philosophies of life. After twenty-five years, I still love and respect him.

Work to develop a positive relationship with your companion. When everything you do is to strengthen the other, you will soon find that you can mutually benefit from your togetherness. You may have numerous differences, but don't be quick to request someone new. You will learn many refining lessons of life while you serve with companions whose personalities differ from yours. Generally you will have only one trainer. In the process of learning all you can from your trainer, take good notes. Chances are that before long you will be asked to train a missionary fresh from the MTC. Do this by using the strong points you learned from your trainer, and make sure you cover areas that your trainer overlooked. From the day you arrive, your mind should be storing information that will make you a better person, missionary, leader, follower, and son or daughter of God.

Your success in learning from your trainer will be reflected not only as you train in the mission but also as you rear your children in years to come. If you become irritated and uncooperative when things don't go as planned, then chances are that you will in effect be tested again until you can teach and lead imperfect followers. You may steadfastly maintain that you will never marry a person who remotely resembles your trainer. True, you can select your mate, but remember that you cannot choose your children. One or more of your children may in some ways be exactly like your trainer! Learn how to work together with your trainer even though you both may be as different as night and day.

"YOU ONLY PASS THIS WAY ONCE"

FOR THOUSANDS OF YEARS AND probably much longer, you have waited to serve your mission. This is your time to be an "angel of the Lord." Elder Heber C. Kimball, a tremendously successful missionary as an apostle of the Lord, said: "While in the act of ministering the Gospel, the servants of God may be considered angels. . . . The servants of God are angels in one sense, sent forth to gather the house of Israel from the four corners of the earth" (in *Journal of Discourses,* 10:103).

When you stop to think that in the Lord's time one day for him equals one thousand years on earth (see Abraham 3:4), we don't have long to serve. In fact, one year for man would be equal to one minute and twenty-six seconds for the Lord. A sister's eighteen-month mission would be two minutes and nine seconds long in the Lord's time. An elder's two-year mission is equivalent to two minutes and fifty-two seconds in the Lord's time. Think of it—less than three minutes to serve an entire mission! At that rate, you'd better get moving. There isn't a minute to waste.

If you keep in mind that sense of urgency all the time, you will not waste time and will thus be able to look back on your mission without regret. Keep in mind that nobody gets a second chance to serve a mission. You might say, "What about when I'm old? Can't I come and serve with my spouse?" Yes, but the circumstances will be entirely different. Now you are young and full of energy. Then you will be old and full of aches and pains. Now you have little or no family responsibility resting on your shoulders. Then you will have not only children but also grandchildren. Now you can enjoy being transferred from place to place with one companion after another. Then you will probably serve in only one area and will definitely keep the same companion for the entire time. Now you are young and can learn the language, scriptures, and discussions easily. Then you will be older, and although you'll have much more experience, the language will sound like garbled noise, the scriptures will be harder to memorize, and the discussions will seem to change every time you open the books to learn them. Now is the time for you to serve.

What difference does it make to you that you will not pass this way again? A big one! You need not be concerned about being shy when talking to people—you will probably never see them again in mortality. If you were to make a total fool of yourself (which you won't), you will never see them again anyway. You may be inspired to visit a struggling member, to help a widow, or to encourage a struggling elders quorum president. If you wait, the opportunity may never be reclaimed. If you wait too long to try new ideas with ward members, you will surely never find out whether those ideas will work. You will not pass this way again.

Opportunities to serve are fleeting. There seem to be windows of time on missions, just as there are in life. For example, the window for serving a mission for most young men is between the ages of nineteen and twenty-six. Unless there are special arrangements, you cannot go earlier and would not be called later. So it goes with life. There is indeed a "season, and a time to every purpose under the heaven" (Ecclesiastes 3:1).

Wandering into your mission without definite goals is the first step toward wasted time. Take time before or soon after you arrive to set some definite, attainable goals. However, one pitfall that entraps many missionaries is trying to live the entire mission on the first day. Take one day at a time.

For those missionaries who feel overwhelmed at the thought of serving for two whole years, just serve today as faithfully as you can. If you want to goof off, plan to do it tomorrow. Of course, when you get up tomorrow it will be today again. But you can still say the same thing: Tomorrow I will kick back and take it easy, but just for today I will be totally diligent. If you live one day at a time, the time will pass quickly and you will still look forward to playtime tomorrow, which will come when the time is right: *after* your mission.

The Savior, knowing how difficult the great tests of life would be and how overwhelming it would be to try to achieve all goals at once, counseled: "Take therefore no thought for the morrow: for the morrow shall take thought for the things of itself. Sufficient unto the day is the evil thereof" (Matthew 6:34).

It was almost humorous to see new elders and sisters at the mission home on the day they arrived to begin their missions. You could tell they thought that the end of their missions would never come. We counseled them to use every moment efficiently because "tomorrow" they would be going home. They would respond with looks of disbelief. But on their last day, as they sat in the mission home and we reviewed their missions, I would remind them of my challenge and note their changed perspective on the duration of their missions. I would say, "Elders and sisters, literally speaking, tomorrow you will be going home! Did you serve as diligently as I challenged you to do on your first day?" What joy came to the hearts of those who could honestly answer yes, and what disappointment came to those who regretfully had to answer no.

Each morning, recommit yourself to serve diligently. Every night before you retire, make plans for the next day. Just do it one day at a time. At first your mission may seem like it will never end, but the longer you have served, the faster the days go by. When the end is finally in sight, you start praying that the time will slow down. Unfortunately, it will not. The last six months are ten times faster than the first six months. You won't fully understand what this means until you experience it.

Some missionaries think that if they are really enjoying themselves and are doing a good job at the end of their missions, the mission president will extend their missions. Don't count on it. The maximum time he can extend your mission (without direct permission from the missionary committee of the Church) is only thirty days.

To help motivate them to make the most of their missions, some missionaries make pacts with friends in other missions that they will be diligent every single day. Others make the same promise to those missionaries who came with them to the same mission—an arrangement that sets an automatic time for them to check up on each other. Five of us elders flew to Samoa together. Four of us finished in Samoa and the fifth finished in Hawaii, but we all checked up on each other at zone conferences. We kept up a little friendly competition—who could memorize the discussions first, who could memorize the most words and scriptures, and who could speak the best. But the real help came every time we met together, because we pumped each other up, encouraged each other, and urged continued diligence. It didn't matter who was "best" or who was called to leadership positions soonest; we only cared about helping the others succeed.

Now is the day of your mission. Perhaps you should mark the joyous invitation that the Lord gave to Thomas B. Marsh in Doctrine and Covenants 31:3: "Lift up your heart and rejoice, *for the hour of your mission is come;* and your tongue shall be loosed, and you shall declare glad tidings of great joy unto this generation" (emphasis added). The saddest missionaries I ever saw were those waiting to board the plane for their return trip who realized they had not served diligently. They thought they were too wise to take counsel from someone as old as a mission president. I saw in those missionaries' faces some of the regret of those who do not live up to their potential in mortality. Now is the time for you to serve! Do it right from the first day to the last.

7

MISSION RULES

WHY ARE THERE SO MANY RULES?" is a question frequently asked by missionaries. It seems like rules cover everything. What's the matter—doesn't the mission president trust you? Nothing could be further from the truth. If you were not a trustworthy person, you would not be called to serve a mission.

Because of your young age and, for many, the rather protected environment you grew up in, the First Presidency and Council of the Twelve have decided to give you rather strict guidelines. If you follow them, they will help you avoid situations that can be spiritually fatal. Some missionaries become disgruntled at seemingly being told everything to do. That is one way to look at it. A different approach might be to stand back in awe at how much Heavenly Father loves you and how "with it" the Brethren really are. In Doctrine and Covenants 38:16 the Lord explains, "And for your salvation I give unto you a commandment, for I have heard your prayers." Earlier in the same section, the Lord cautioned the early elders: "Behold, the enemy is combined. And now I show unto you a mystery, a thing which is had in secret chambers, to bring to pass even your destruction in process of time, and ye knew it not" (verses 12–13).

The devil will never let you go unnoticed or unchallenged. From the many accounts written by missionaries, I have marveled that the Lord has so constantly watched over his missionaries. Some missionaries were warned to flee their apartments in the middle of the night. Others were prompted to stay at a member's home longer than usual, thus avoiding physical harm from a pending disaster. Others have talked about being prompted to leave investigators' homes, take alternative routes, or make phone calls that interrupted suicide attempts—and the list goes on.

Very often it is not evident at the time why we are prompted to do certain things. People may laugh and mock our attempts to be sensitive to the Spirit. Sometimes we never find out what the Lord was protecting us from. Other times we learn why we behaved as we did. Given the number of missionaries who have recorded how they on occasion did not heed the promptings of the Spirit and then suffered as a result, I have a firm testimony that the Lord's promised blessings—including those of protective watch care (see D&C 84:42, 88)—are more surely with us, as he says, "when ye do what I say" (D&C 82:10).

Sometimes we may feel we are being treated as little children because instructions often come without explanations. Father Adam set a godly example for us:

> And Adam and Eve, his wife, called upon the name of the Lord, and they heard the voice of the Lord from the way toward the Garden of Eden, speaking unto them, and they saw him not; for they were shut out from his presence.
>
> And he gave unto them commandments, that they should worship the Lord their God, and should offer the firstlings of their flocks, for an offering unto the

Lord. And Adam was obedient unto the commandments of the Lord.

And after many days an angel of the Lord appeared unto Adam, saying: Why dost thou offer sacrifices unto the Lord? And Adam said unto him: I know not, save the Lord commanded me (Moses 5:4–6).

Our grand patriarch did not feel that an explanation of the reason behind the commandments was necessary for him to obey. The scriptural phrase "after many days" often denotes the passage of many years. We should be more faithful. Adam knew that God did not frivolously command anything. Because he had perfect faith in God, he obeyed. Since we have enough faith to come on missions, shouldn't we exercise faith and obey the rules until the Lord helps us understand?

If you really struggle with a rule, obey it until you can receive a clarification. Ask other missionaries if they know why that rule was given. If they don't know, ask the president in one of your weekly letters or during an interview. Often a light will turn on when you see the rationale behind the rule. I have heard so many times, "President, I had never looked at it that way before!" However, even if you receive what seems to you to be an unsatisfactory answer, you are not authorized to break the rule.

Perhaps an illustration will help. On page twenty-one of the *Missionary Handbook,* under the heading "Letter Writing," you will read, "Do not carry on any unauthorized communication, by phone or letter, with individuals (including members) within or close to your mission boundaries." Later, on page twenty-five, the handbook continues: "You are not to telephone, write to, or accept calls or letters from anyone of the opposite sex living within or near mission boundaries." From your point of view that may seem rather silly. Naturally, you have become close to members and investigators in other areas. To you the rule may seem illogical. Consider just a few of the implications from a mission president's point of view. You are a part of a set of missionaries who are well liked and have many close friends in a particular area. When you and your companion leave that area, there is an automatic resistance to change, so the new missionaries may not be welcomed as warmly as they could be. If there is a telephone dialogue between you and the members, the friendship and support for the new missionaries may be delayed for many weeks. You then become responsible for those who should have been taught and contacted but were not because the new missionaries never gained trust in the area.

Now for the other edge of the sword. While you are calling, writing, and thinking about your former area, you cannot devote your undivided attention to the new area. You cannot serve with "all your heart, might, mind and strength," because you are working less than you could in the new area. You will have to account also for those people you failed to contact and teach in the new area. Add to that the fact that you have openly disobeyed mission rules, and this, to a degree, deprives you of a fulness of the Spirit. Without that, you will miss promptings you otherwise might have enjoyed. Lessons for the present and future will go unlearned, and everyone will suffer. It is also possible that your companion will see your disobedience and use your example to justify breaking mission rules. The members may hear you talk and realize you are not obedient. They don't want their family and friends taught by a disobedient missionary, so they withhold their investigator until a new, more obedient missionary comes to the area. The ball rolls on and on, and the work does not prosper as it should.

The rules are given for your protection. On pages twenty-two and twenty-three, under the title "Recreational and Cultural Activities," the handbook cautions against engaging in "contact sports, water sports, winter sports, motorcycling, horseback riding, mountain climbing, riding in private boats or airplanes, handling firearms or explosives of any kind, or similar activities. Never go swimming. You may play basketball but not full court or in organized leagues or tournaments." What a list! Each of those activities could be discussed at length. The wisdom behind most missionary rules is evident.

Regarding sports activities, it is important that missionaries avoid losing their tempers. Many missions have banned basketball because one or two missionaries failed to control their tempers. More than once, reports came to the mission office of investigators who discontinued taking the discussions because some immature, hot-headed missionary acted like a little kid on the basketball court. How much is the worth of a soul? If you uncontrollably lose your temper when you play, then be adult enough not to play. Think how it might feel trying to explain to the Savior how you allowed yourself to drive someone away from investigating the gospel by your unsportsmanlike conduct.

Every mission has stories about the tragic effects of missionaries who failed to live by the rules. Sometimes the consequences are only the destruction of a mission car or a bicycle, but other times, injury or death is the result of careless actions. Whatever the consequences, when the missionaries go down, the work is not done. Does it matter if you choose to disobey only a few rules? The Lord counseled, "No man receiveth a fulness unless he keepeth [God's] commandments" (D&C 93:27). It is hypocrisy of the worst kind to teach people to listen and obey if you listen and choose to disobey. If you are going to represent the Lord, do so by first keeping all his rules and commandments.

One of the most frequently used excuses is "Everybody else breaks the rule." Is that supposed to justify your actions? In the early days of this dispensation, the Lord chastised the Prophet Joseph Smith by saying: "Behold, you should not have feared man more than God. Although men set at naught the counsels of God, and despise his words—yet you should have been faithful" (D&C 3:7–8).

The happy missionary is the faithful, obedient missionary. There is never any fear in him or her. So what if the mission president makes a surprise visit? The obedient missionary will always be found doing what he or she is supposed to do. What if the Savior came personally or sent an angel for a visual account of what you are doing? There's no problem if you are obedient. If you are not, there will always be fear of being caught or embarrassment for not doing what you have promised. You cannot have the peace and confidence the Lord has promised to the faithful and obedient unless you do what is asked.

One of the greatest favors you can do for yourself, your future family, your companion, the mission, and the Lord is to decide, before you enter the mission, to follow Nephi's example of obedience. The Lord has promised that he will open the way for you to accomplish what he has commanded you (see 1 Nephi 3:7). Happy indeed is the missionary who can sit in the president's office for the exit interview and truthfully report having been totally obedient for the entire time he or she served.

8

···········

LEARNING A LANGUAGE—
FOREIGN OR ENGLISH

WHAT A THRILL IT WAS WHEN you opened your mission call and saw you were expected to learn a new language. What a frightening experience it was when the thrill wore off and you realized it was entirely up to you whether you learned to speak this language well or not. Despite the many doubts the adversary plants in your mind about your ability to learn a new language, remember that the Lord did not call you to fail. If you do all you can, he will make up for any lack of ability and preparation on your part.

Your MTC experience may have even convinced you that while learning the rudiments of a language is one thing, achieving a comfortable level of proficiency is perhaps too difficult for you. Or you may mistakenly believe that what you learned at the MTC made you an expert in your new language. Neither view is correct. One of those unmistakable revelations happens the day you arrive to your mission area. You may think you know the language well enough, but when the local people speak it, it may be entirely different from what your instructors spoke at the MTC.

So here you are in your mission, perhaps doubting your ability to master the language. Where do you go from here?

Be assured: Learning another language really isn't as difficult as it may appear. Take it a little at a time. Be confident that the Lord will help you learn the language well enough to fulfill his divine purposes.

Set a language-study schedule that is reasonable and achievable. It would be wonderful if you could study all day long, every day until you have mastered the language. Realistically, you will never have enough time to feel completely comfortable in your studies for the gospel still must be preached and people need to be contacted, helped, and loved.

If you are blessed with a native missionary as a trainer, your enunciation of the language will be helped, but your knowledge of grammatical structure will suffer. Many natives do not know why they speak as they do any more than you know why you speak English as you do. On the other hand, if you have an English-speaking companion, your questions about grammar will be answered, but your ability to speak like a native will develop more slowly.

The first reaction to learning a language is generally enthusiasm and energy—you can hardly wait to get into the language. The second reaction, which generally comes within a couple of weeks, is one of frustration and discouragement. At this point too many missionaries resign themselves to mediocrity in speaking the language. For example, they may find it too difficult to learn all the rules concerning masculine and feminine articles and verb tenses. It may not seem worth the effort to learn the "respect language" and all the flowery, poetic ways people say things. Rationalizing may go on and on, a sign that the missionary is unwilling to strive for excellence in the language.

The choice is up to you. You can tell yourself how hard

you've got it and how nobody understands your trials. You may feel you have earned the right to become depressed. You may even mistakenly believe that the Lord has called you to the wrong mission. But at that very point of frustration, you can also choose to roll up your sleeves and master the language.

Break the task down into small, bite-sized pieces. Don't try to learn everything at once. Many missionaries have successfully learned languages by setting a realistic goal of learning ten words a day for the first year of their mission. That would give you a working vocabulary nearly as large as you normally use in English. You may find that you can handle more than ten words a day, or maybe you will have to settle for seven or eight words. Whatever the goal, write down the words on index cards and go over and over them every day until you can use them confidently. Say them to members, to little kids on the street, to your companion, and to your investigators. If they laugh at you, don't be offended—a little sense of humor on your part goes a long way in keeping things in proper perspective.

Learn how to say common phrases you need to use every day. You can easily do this by thinking of the phrase in English and then having your companion (or preferably a native speaker) translate it into the language. If you learn five phrases each day, in a month you will have fair mastery of the "chitchat" language. By the end of the second month, you could develop more advanced speaking skills. By the end of the third month, you should be able to say just about anything you need to say. By the end of the sixth month, the natives will marvel at your ability to express yourself.

Many missionaries and members gained their testimony by reading the Book of Mormon. A great many missionaries found that reading the Book of Mormon out loud in the new language was also a key to increasing their vocabulary and their general fluency. There seems to be something magical about the Book of Mormon. It blesses whoever embraces it, spiritually and intellectually. Use the power of that great book to learn to speak well. Have your companion, a member, or an investigator listen to you read. Not only will it help you in your conversational skills, but it will also help strengthen that person's testimony. I know of missionaries who practiced this technique with their investigators until the day they finished their missions. Remember, when the Spirit comes, your mind will be enlightened, your soul will be filled with joy, and you can know all things by the power of the Spirit (see D&C 11:13–14).

Don't overlook the power of testimony. As our daughter learned French, she wanted more than anything to share her testimony with the people. Her vocabulary was a limiting factor. As she struggled to express herself, in the spirit of helpfulness the people would supply the words she was searching for. The Spirit, the true converter, bore testimony to the people that the words they were helping her with were true. Her sincerity and willingness to try to share her testimony only added to the spirituality of the experience. Even after learning the language, she would ask them to help correct her structure and pronunciation because their involvement opened them up to the testimony of the Spirit.

There seems to be something necessary about hearing your own voice speak in a foreign language. As I learned to speak Samoan on my first mission, I got so I could read perfectly to myself. It wasn't until I tried to read out loud to my companion that my tongue got all tied in knots and I sounded like a baby making strange, nonsensical sounds.

As quickly as you are able, say all of your prayers in your new language; the Lord understands, even if your companion doesn't. Force yourself to speak exclusively in your new language around the apartment and as you proselyte—it will greatly increase your linguistic ability. If you slip back into English whenever you want to, you just postpone the time when you can effectively communicate in your new language.

Above all, don't get uptight! The more you tell yourself you "can't," the more of a self-fulfilling prophecy you become. When your mind feels "fried," take a break. It is much easier to learn when you are fresh and not quite so frustrated. Don't make any snap judgments. You may decide after just a couple of weeks that you are not cut out to serve in a foreign land and that you need to be reassigned to an English-speaking mission. However, if you quit trying, you will miss some of the sweetest experiences of your life.

LEARNING "GOSPEL ENGLISH"

Foreign language missions are exciting and challenging, and English-speaking missions are equally enjoyable. The most important factor is not whether you learn a new language but how effectively you can present the gospel to your investigators. Speaking by the power of the Spirit in any language is one of the most thrilling experiences a missionary can have.

If you are a native English speaker and are assigned to an English-speaking mission, you may feel like you don't have a language to learn. That isn't exactly correct. Too many people grow up using slang, trendy, ungrammatical, imprecise, or otherwise unclear language. Your friends may understand you well enough, but the people you are teaching may not. Language is like a car. It is the vehicle used to transport your thoughts and ideas. Although an old clunker car may (or may not!) get you to your destination, the people who observe you may be turned off by your mode of transportation. You may feel that they are being judgmental and that they need to correct their attitude. You may even be right—but you are there to teach them the gospel so they can correct their attitudes according to divinely revealed principles. If you cannot gain their trust and respect so that you can communicate effectively with them, they will never be able to adjust their attitudes or, much more important, gain a testimony of the gospel.

Ask someone who speaks English well to critique your language. It may be a surprise to discover how many inappropriate words and phrases you use. Working with your companion, determine to overcome the "language barrier." Language usage varies from country to country and from one area to another. Words and gestures that are meaningless or clever in one country may have vulgar or otherwise negative connotations in another country. Be sensitive to language usage wherever you go. Avoid learning slang and swear words. A representative of the Savior should shun such "telestial" language.

Learning "gospel English" is no easy task. The words and phrases used in religious discussions may be new and (at first) uncomfortable. Practice until you can explain gospel principles in language your investigators can understand. You will discover, like the thousands who have gone before you, that teaching concepts familiar to you but brand-new to investigators is extremely demanding. Any distractions caused by your language, unfamiliarity with the proper words, inappropriate gestures, or mispronunciations may increase the effort needed to bring investigators to understanding. Deliberately showing off by using words that investigators may not understand is childish at best. With his perfect intellect, the Savior could have used words and concepts that even the most intelligent would not have understood. However, he often chose to teach in simple terms so that humble people of all stations could understand (see D&C 1:24; 133:57–58).

Practice using language that is interesting and precise. Learn to say exactly what you mean. There will always be people who are waiting to make you an "offender for a word" (Isaiah 29:21). Being aware of "politically correct" and tactful language is challenging even for the professional. Until investigators and members are convinced that you have their best interests at heart, they are more critical of the language you use. Listening closely to the language people use will direct alert missionaries on how cautious they must be in the words they choose.

Be teachable. If someone corrects you because you use, for example, a sexist term, thank the person and make the change. Only in rare cases will a person be so demanding regarding "political correctness" that you cannot present your message. Perhaps that person's time to hear the gospel is yet in the future and your time could be more productively used with people who are more interested in the message than in the language.

Language is fun and exciting whether you speak English or use a foreign language on your mission. By giving attention to the words you use, you can provide a fertile environment where the Holy Ghost can carry your message to the hearts of the listener in a way that shifts the responsibility for the burden of the message from your shoulders to theirs. Nephi taught, "When a man speaketh by the power of the

Holy Ghost the power of the Holy Ghost carrieth it *unto the hearts* of the children of men" (2 Nephi 33:1; emphasis added).

As you progress towards godliness during your mission in so many attributes and characteristics, make sure you include language. Remember the Lord's pattern on how to tell whether a person is from God or Satan: "He that speaketh, whose spirit is contrite, whose language is meek and edifieth, the same is of God if he obey mine ordinances" (D&C 52:16).

9

·········

KINDERGARTEN DECISIONS

IT SEEMS A BIT STRANGE TO TALK about making "kindergarten decisions" on a mission. Don't get the wrong impression of the content of this chapter. What is a kindergarten decision? The words alone suggest simple basic decisions that are easy to make and easy to follow. The decisions we discuss in this chapter are indeed simple to make, but they are much more challenging to follow. The advantage of making a kindergarten decision once and then never having to make it again is that you free up all your energy to live your commitment. Perhaps an example would explain this more clearly.

Before you ever left the MTC, you decided to obey all mission rules. The first rule you face every morning is to get up at the designated time. It sounds so simple to honor that rule, but many missionaries struggle every day in that area. Make up your mind only once that you will be up on time, whether you feel well or sick or tired or discouraged or anything else.

You'll find that without this resolve to be obedient something interesting happens five minutes before the alarm clock goes off. That soft, comfortable mattress that has cuddled you all night suddenly turns vicious. It weighs about five hundred pounds and somehow is on top of you, pinning you to the box springs! Try as you may, it continues to smother you until fifteen or twenty minutes past the designated wake-up time.

Another revelation that hopefully you will not have to learn the hard way is that the difference between 6:30 A.M. and 6:45 A.M. is a lot more than just fifteen minutes. At 6:30 A.M. you can arise with confidence and ask for the blessings of heaven on your day. At 6:45 A.M. you feel like you have cheated the Lord and would be acting hypocritically to ask for blessings, because you haven't fulfilled your promise to get up on time. I have listened to elders and sisters lament over an entirely ruined day because they slept through the alarm.

Of course, you will encounter those who scoff at your decision to get up on time, but those who scoff are not getting up on time themselves. One of the true ironies of the mission is that those who break the rules always jeer the loudest at those who try to fulfill the promises that scoffers too have made. Let me broaden that concept just a little: the only ones who mock you for serving a mission are those who have never served. Those who play down the importance of temple marriage are those who have not sacrificed to be married there. People who poke fun at those who are trying to live a celestial life in this world are those who have quit trying.

If you think it will be easy to get up on time every morning, you're mistaken! There will be times when extenuating circumstances will keep you up past bedtime; for example, if you have been out late administering to an investigator or member and didn't get to bed until 2:00 A.M. You may be tempted to rationalize your sleeping in in order to make up for a few hours of lost sleep. There may be days when you feel sick and know you'll just be back in bed anyway. The challenge is to be true to your kindergarten decision. Get up and take a shower, study for a while, and then if you need to go back to bed because of sickness, you will not feel guilty about letting the Lord down or going back on your commitment to yourself.

Anytime you decide to do something worthwhile, the devil is aware of it. He redoubles his efforts to try to make you fail. Even responsibilities that were not a problem before become real challenges during the mission. Many missionaries who served with us came from farming areas where getting up at 6:30 A.M. seemed like sleeping in; they were accustomed to arising as early as 4:00 A.M. But as the months rolled by, they would find it was just as difficult to get up at 6:30 A.M. as it used to be at 4:00 A.M. Indeed, making the decision is the easy part. Following through on the commitment requires all the dedication you can muster.

What other decisions fall into this category? You may come up with a whole list of them, but I will list a few that missionaries have shared with me.

Getting out of the apartment on time every day. On P days there is no problem, nor on Sundays—it's the regular day that seems so taxing. There is always a last-minute phone call to make, a last entry on the daily planner, dishes to do, a letter to the president to finish. The list is endless, and the result is always the same if you give in—you're late getting out.

Not staying longer than an hour at a dinner appointment. Members love to have you in their homes and are willing to incur the additional expense of feeding two missionaries with bottomless stomachs. They like the spirit they feel when you are around. They like to talk to you, have you sing with the family, enjoy a casual conversation—they have a thousand other reasons for detaining you. Although they mean well, they must realize that the sharp, spiritual cutting edge of your mission will be dulled if you stay longer than allowed. The wife doesn't mean to delay you, but the meal is late and dinner doesn't start until the hour is almost over. But if you have made the right kindergarten decision, you will excuse yourself and go "knock on a few doors" for another half hour before the meal is served. It will be impressive and instructive to the family when they see your dedication and diligence. Try to have an appointment set for an hour and fifteen minutes after the start of the meal. That will help you leave on time.

Deciding to finish the day's work on time—not early, not late. It is always difficult to gauge when a discussion will end, but coming in late by an hour or more should be a rare exception. One of the finest elders who ever served with us was one who always made excuses about why he couldn't get in on time. I worked with him for his entire mission. At one critical point I told him that although I wanted to make him a leader, I couldn't hold him up as an example if he continued to come in late. He agreed to change and did for a month or so. I called him to be a zone leader, and he was doing well until reports started coming from his zone members and also from his companion that he was coming in late again.

I called him in and discussed the problem with him. He vowed to do better. He did for a few days, then was back to the habit. An opening came for another assistant to the president. By all rights he should have been the pick, but I chose another elder who was more diligent in keeping the rules. The offending elder and I had a good discussion, during which he said he understood why I couldn't choose him. He again vowed to change, but he didn't.

At the end of his mission, I drove him to the airport. We rode along in silence for a few miles, and then he said to me, "President, I've been thinking. I don't think my staying out late was such a bad thing. I know a lot of elders who do a lot worse than that!" I prayed hard for the right answer to help this elder understand. Like a bolt of lightning from the great beyond, the answer came. I said, "Elder, what you say is true. The rule you continuously broke was not a big one. But answer me one question. How many rules do you think Jesus could have broken before he disqualified himself from being the Savior?" The effect was dramatic and immediate. Of course, we are not perfect like the Savior, but he has asked us to be perfect (see 3 Nephi 12:48)—a state we will not attain until we learn to be perfectly obedient, among other things. We may repent of our disobedience and make it to the celestial kingdom, but what blessings and growth opportunities will we have forfeited because we were unwilling to obey the little rules? Maybe that will be part of our punishment on the other side of the veil—seeing what we could have enjoyed had we been a bit more diligent. Don't excuse your disobedience!

Writing a weekly letter to the president every P day. It is easy to believe that the president won't miss your letter, since probably two hundred other missionaries also write every week. If you want the mission president to receive inspiration for you, then provide him with information. It is true: "Inspiration works better on information than on perspiration." Let the president use his limited time and energy to find solutions to your stated problems rather than try to figure out what your problems are. It always amused me to talk to elders and sisters who thought I could see into their lives as through a crystal ball and identify their problems. Yes, sometimes the Spirit would let me know what the problems were, but often the Lord seemed to say, "If they want help, let them ask. Then I'll inspire you to help them solve their problems." Even if you are the only one in the apartment who takes a few minutes to report your stewardship to your priesthood leader, you will receive the blessings.

Writing a weekly letter to your parents. Just decide once, and then "do it." You will discover, like all diligent missionaries, that there just isn't enough time on P day to write everybody who wants to hear from you. Unfortunately, even girlfriends and boyfriends take a back seat after you have been out for a few months. Whether you are close to your parents or not, you owe them a letter. Your letters will bless their lives and also provide an excellent record of your mission. You may rationalize however you want, but to be totally obedient requires that you make this kindergarten decision once and follow through on that decision every week.

Holding daily companionship study. This is yet another decision that is easy to make and difficult to follow. During the early months of your mission, you will have a trainer who will try hard to get you started right. After you have been out awhile, it is easy to rationalize that you learn more from individual study than you do with your companion as a study partner. Perhaps you should remember the Lord's promise in Doctrine and Covenants 6:32: "Where two or three are gathered together in my name, as touching one thing, behold, there will I be in the midst of them—even so am I in the midst of you." As spiritual as you are and as laid back as your companion may be, you alone do not qualify as "two or three." Why deprive yourself of the promised presence of the Lord because you may impulsively believe it is a "pain" to study with your companion? Just decide to be obedient, and then use the rest of your energy in following through on your commitment. The results will surprise you and your companion as you increase your gospel knowledge as well as become more unified in spirit and testimony with your companion.

I could go on page after page about decisions that are easy to make, difficult to start, and worthwhile to keep. These decisions make the difference between being an excellent missionary or just being an ordinary or mediocre missionary. And with a little imagination, you readily can see how this kind of experience—sharing ideas, working together toward a common goal, and getting along with others—will prepare you for marriage and a career.

10
....

KEEPING YOUR EYE SINGLE
TO GOD'S GLORY

FOR THE FAIR PORTION OF THE first nineteen or twenty-one years of your life, you likely have focused at different times on things such as school, dating, cars, sports, fun, jobs, and yourself. Yet now, almost overnight, you are expected to focus on God, scriptures, service, missionary work, helping members, sharing the gospel, and striving for eternal life. Sometimes the shock seems almost too much to handle.

It is by far the "easy route" to just talk about whatever you want to talk about while you are in your apartment or between appointments. While that may be the easy thing to do, it certainly is not the most spiritually productive or obedient thing to do.

If you continually bring up worldly things, it is much more difficult to concentrate on spiritual things. Unless you are really on the ball, you could spend two years away from home and never receive the blessings of serving a mission. When missionaries try to keep one foot in Babylon and the other foot in the mission field, they become frustrated, and will never be completely happy in either. One can't serve two masters!

Because it can be difficult to focus on the mission all the

time, some missionaries give up trying to do that. Those who willingly pay the price find that the rewards far outweigh the costs. How do you do it? Begin on the first day of your companionship. Sit down with your companion and decide that you want to experience the positive effects of 100 percent focus on the work. As you have extra time between teaching appointments, pick a topic and discuss it. You will find the Topical Guide in your English version of the King James Bible to be a great source of discussion subjects. Pick a doctrine of the week and encourage everyone in the apartment to learn all they can about it. Review the questions that people ask about the subject. Investigate the subject from every direction you can think of. Prepare talks or thoughts about it. Defend it from the scriptures. Outline your thoughts. As you begin to use your free time efficiently, your hunger to study the word of God will increase dramatically. You can hardly wait to get home and study or meet with other missionaries to see what they have learned. Rapidly you will gain the reputation of being the "mission scholar." You will humbly discover that although you have learned many new things in your mission, there remains an infinite amount that you do not know. Your desire to learn will grow and grow until you become immersed in the gospel. That is when insights come and answers to prayers become more distinct.

The time will pass so quickly that you'll sense the urgency of the work and will labor tirelessly to spread the gospel to everyone you can. Lest you think that I am a dreamer and that such commitment never happens, know that I am painfully aware of how few missionaries take the challenge. However, those who do focus on the gospel will testify that everything I've said here is correct.

Perhaps you need to start off more slowly than the pace I've indicated. If that is the case, attack one portion of your "free time." Maybe you and your companion choose to focus during the day between meetings on doctrines of the gospel. After doing that for a few weeks, you can suggest that you expand your efforts to include time spent in the apartment. Once your companion tastes the meat, he will never again be satisfied with the milk.

Unfortunately, one of the real challenges is the members with good intentions who want to know about your premission past and your postmission plans. They want a detailed account of how your girlfriend or boyfriend is doing. They want to know about your interests, your hobbies, your college major, your family, and on and on. Perhaps they bring these things up because they are not very comfortable discussing the gospel with you. That is where you need to take the lead. Offer to lead a discussion on a topic you are currently studying. Give the members an opportunity to ask and answer questions about the gospel. The Spirit will come into the discussion, and before long they will want you to come all the time because they love the feeling that comes when you discuss spiritual things with them.

A few members are far enough away from the Spirit that they will feel uncomfortable if you constantly want to share a spiritual experience or thought with them. Keep working with them as long as you can to try to help them improve, but keep your guard up. If you see no progress with the members, try to have the home teachers perform more of that fellowshipping role, while you move on to more productive work.

In building relationships of trust with members and nonmembers, a certain amount of sharing of backgrounds is essential. You must be sensitive to the Spirit to know when enough common ground has been laid and it is time to help them take the next spiritual step forward. The Spirit is there when you talk about spiritual things, read the scriptures, and discuss the gospel.

You will discover a need to grow into the principle of discussing the gospel nearly all the time—as often as is appropriate and helpful. Once your reputation is established, you will find that others will try to help you focus, even if they are not willing to do so themselves. Avoid the temptation to show off your newfound knowledge; no one likes a know-it-all. If you come across that way, people will turn away from you, and then what good is your knowledge? Once you have established yourself as a serious gospel scholar, others will seek opportunities to discuss the gospel with you. When they ask you questions, you can bet that they are sincerely interested in what you have to say. Only when you find yourself continually volunteering information will you find others turning away from you. Give others a chance to share their ideas.

It happens naturally and doesn't take very long that those who like intensified learning seek each other out. That shouldn't surprise you, since the scriptures clearly teach that "likes attract" (see D&C 88:40). Make sure you don't exclude those who are just starting to catch the study bug—everyone has to start somewhere. Also, if your learning becomes too specialized, you will find that you know more and more about less and less until you are no good to anyone but yourself. Avoid "gospel hobbyhorses," those topics that seem of themselves to become "the Gospel" for the unwise. Some of those topics are the Word of Wisdom, making your calling and election sure, and the Second Comforter. Yes, they are all part of the true doctrine of Christ, but they are only part. Do not allow yourself to become involved in gospel study groups with overly enthusiastic members. That is not your calling.

Stick with basic doctrine. Faith is the most profound and least understood doctrine of the gospel, and a close second is repentance. If you want to define what should be your first eight topics for study, look at 3 Nephi 27:13–22, where the Savior defines what he refers to as "my gospel." To make it somewhat easier to get started in your study, those eight foundational doctrines are (1) atonement, (2) resurrection, (3) judgment, (4) faith in Christ, (5) repentance, (6) baptism, (7) Holy Ghost, and (8) enduring to the end.

As you enlarge and broaden your understanding of those eight doctrines, you will find that the gospel is one beautifully intertwined whole—every part inseparably connected with the others. My experience suggests that a careful investigation of those eight doctrines could easily occupy more of your free time than you have during an eighteen-month or two-year mission. So don't be so anxious to delve into the thick of thin topics.

As you meet with others who are also determined to increase their understanding of the gospel, quiz each other. Instead of just using the lazy way of referring constantly to the "hearsay gospel," require a reference on each point you make. If you are not familiar with the "hearsay gospel," it goes something like this: "I heard that Elder McConkie said . . ." Someone then asks: "Where did he say that?" To which the lazy scholar will say, "I don't know, but I'm sure he said it!" Discount as hearsay everything that cannot be documented. Even now, as a full-time teacher, if I don't know the reference for a statement, I will say, "Just count it as hearsay until I can document it."

It is very helpful to use the living prophets and the scriptures as a guide. If they say little or nothing about a topic, be wise to do the same. Using them as a guide will keep you on safe ground doctrinally not only while you are serving a mission but for the rest of your life.

Finally, take the advice of your mission president. Even though you may be having the time of your life, if he thinks you are going too far in study, back off. He is there to keep Satan from taking advantage of your youthful enthusiasm. The only missionaries who get into trouble are those who will not heed warnings. Keep the president informed about what you are doing. He will encourage you and give you the necessary guidelines to be especially effective.

11
....

USING YOUR FINANCES WISELY

FOR SOME MISSIONARIES, THE monthly living allowance will be more money than they have ever had to spend; for others it will seem like poverty. Whether you fit on one end of the continuum or the other or somewhere in between, the money you receive each month comes from the consecrated funds of the Church. You may say, "No, my parents pay the money to the ward every month, and the clerk forwards it to me." Not so. Your parents or others may donate a certain amount of money every month into the missionary account of the ward, but once that donation is made, both you and your parents lose control of where it goes, because it is a free-will offering. From the missionary account in the ward, the Church deducts a certain amount for each missionary serving from that ward. The Church in turn distributes from its central missionary fund enough money to cover the expenses of each missionary according to where he or she is serving. If you are serving in the South Pacific, the expenses may be fairly low. If you are serving in England, Japan, or Alaska, the monthly requirement may be much larger. No matter where you serve, you will receive according to your needs, as determined by the mission president working with the individual missionaries.

If you have been blessed to learn early in life how to use

your money wisely, you will find mission finances to be a rather pleasant experience. If, however, you did not learn to discipline yourself during adolescence, then mission finances can be a painful learning experience. The one curveball thrown to even the best-prepared missionary is a companion who is not wise in the use of his or her funds.

Usually the normal operating expenses (housing, utilities, phone) are taken out of your allotment before you even see it. That makes it much easier for you, because the mission president is able to equalize those costs among all the missionaries. If that isn't the case, you may have a real shock. If you happen to serve in an area where the housing is expensive, you will find that the amount you can spend on food will decrease because of the higher rent you pay. Although you are expected to be conservative in your spending habits, you are not expected to go without food, shelter, clothing or other essentials. If the amount you receive just does not cover the costs, what do you do?

First, talk to the other missionaries and find out how they are making it. It may be that you must now learn some of the painful but necessary money-management lessons of life. Eventually (in marriage) you will appreciate this type of training, but while you are going through it, it is not very pleasant. Look at where you spend your money; for a couple of months, keep a detailed account of everything you spend. Then sit down and see where the holes are in your budget. Are you buying a lot of junk food? Are you eating out at fast-food restaurants too often? Are you spending money on nonessentials like souvenirs, cameras, or luxury items? Since you will probably be asked to pay for all unauthorized long-distance phone calls, are you making calls that could be (and should be) eliminated? Are you buying things and sending packages home for family or special friends, thereby using consecrated funds for things for which those funds were not intended? Even in Book of Mormon days, Jacob counseled the people: "Do not spend money for that which is of no worth, nor your labor for that which cannot satisfy" (2 Nephi 9:51). That was good advice then, and it is good advice now.

How do you learn to spend wisely? Put first things first. Make a list of the essentials, those things you must pay for whether you like it or not: housing, utilities, telephone expenses, fast offerings, bus passes—any expense (unless already taken out by the mission office) that occurs every month. Then set aside a little money for emergencies. If you don't budget, you stand a good chance of always being in the hole. Life is full of emergencies. A bike tire blows out, a dog tears your suit pants, your scriptures are lost or stolen, or an unexpected transfer (midmonth) requires transportation costs. Just plan for emergencies. Keep a reserve on hand. How much? Ask direction from your mission president, because each mission will be different. An Australian mission that extends 2,500 miles from one end to the other will require more than a California mission that is sandwiched between four freeways and can be crossed in forty-five minutes.

Plan for other necessities that are not readily used up but in time must be replaced. Cleaners for the apartment, dishwashing soap, laundry detergent, stamps, stationery, toiletries, replacement clothing—all must figure into this fund. You must determine how much it will cost in an *average* month and then stick to that figure. Don't be so shortsighted that you figure you have the money to spend just because it is sitting in your bank account.

Finally, you must plan for food. It is critical to plan for

the entire month. One method is to divide the remaining money (after deducting all of the above items) into four parts. If you have ready access to the money in your bank account, leave most of it there. Take out only enough food money for that week. If you don't have ready access to a bank account, put the money into four separate envelopes. Label one for each of the four weeks in the month, and then don't touch it before that week. It is sad when a missionary calls up early in the month and says that he is completely out of money. Short-term loans from the mission are possible, but they still must be paid back within a couple of months—it isn't free money.

As the weeks go on, you will get a feel for how you are spending your money. Perhaps you buy a lot of food right after transfers because you know you will not move for at least another month. If everyone in the apartment is buying together, make sure everyone pays his or her fair share. It causes harsh feelings when someone freeloads on the rest. If you all decide to do the bulk of your buying right after transfers, you may find that you spend more than one-fourth of your allotment for food during that first week. It is unwise to spend the entire monthly amount at one time, no matter how you plan it out. Why? Because milk, vegetables, bread, and other perishables will not keep for the entire month! Sour milk doesn't taste very good on cold cereal.

If you happen to be in an apartment with someone who is very conservative about spending money, it may be wise to buy your food separately and prepare your own food, thereby keeping the peace by eliminating that possible area of conflict. If you happen to be the conservative one, don't try to impose your thrifty attitudes on everyone else. The conflict will come when everyone in the apartment decides to go out to eat and one person is unwilling because of his or her attitude toward thrift. Those are problems to resolve during a companionship inventory. The solution is not for the more generous companion to "always" avoid eating out, or for the conservative companion to "always" have to eat out with the others. Compromise is possible and desirable.

For those of you serving in foreign lands, it is very possible that your native companions will be much more careful about spending money than you are accustomed to. Sometimes it requires some creativity to solve the problems. For example, if cleared by the mission leadership and agreeable to all concerned, you might team up with a different companion on a P day so that the two of you who want (maybe need) to eat out can do that, while those who see no value in it can do some other fun activity with someone who shares a similar philosophy. Be careful not to give the impression that your companion is cheap. It is not worth bad feelings just because you differ in spending philosophies. Paul gave some timely advice to the Romans (who must have liked to eat out a lot):

> Let not him that eateth despise him that eateth not; and let not him which eateth not judge him that eateth: for God hath received him. . . .
>
> But if thy brother be grieved with thy meat, now walkest thou not charitably. Destroy not him with thy meat, for whom Christ died. . . .
>
> For the kingdom of God is not meat and drink; but righteousness, and peace, and joy in the Holy Ghost . . .
>
> It is good neither to eat flesh, nor to drink wine, nor anything whereby thy brother stumbleth, or is offended, or is made weak. . . .

Let every one of us please his neighbor for his good to edification (Romans 14:3, 15, 17, 21; 15:2).

Follow the white handbook in not lending money to or borrowing money from other missionaries, members, or nonmembers. If you have budgeted, kept a close record, and been wise in your spending and still find that you do not have sufficient for your needs, contact the mission president. The Lord does not expect you to starve or jeopardize your health while you serve your mission. Funds are available to assure safe, sanitary housing and sufficient food.

It is a temptation to write home for extra funds if you run short. *Don't do it.* The Church has asked each mission to determine a fair and equitable amount necessary to support each missionary. When you receive extra money from home (on a regular basis), it becomes impossible to determine what is needed to survive. Look beyond yourself. Your family may be able to afford a few extra dollars a month, but what about those families who cannot? By writing home for extra money, you place an unfair burden on those who serve with and follow you. When the equalized funding program was initiated, we were asked to establish a base and try to live on it for a year. The next year we reevaluated the costs to see if we needed to increase or decrease the allotment. We were able to do that with few problems, because the missionaries had caught the vision of what Church leaders were trying to do and had diligently tried to live within the allotted amount. Our needed increase was easily justified because of diligent bookkeeping on the part of the missionaries. You will be asked to participate in the same process because of the changing nature of economics around the world. Don't let down those who follow you.

What about gifts of money from home? Be grateful for

such generous people. You are not at present asked to return surplus funds to the mission, but someday that may be requested. For now, be sensitive not to flaunt your extra money before those who don't have it. Don't make money a central issue during your mission, because you only need to take care of the basic needs. Gifts sent to you while you are serving your mission are increase and should be tithed through your home ward.

Make sure you do not use the consecrated funds (that which you receive from the mission) to lend to members or investigators. There are other channels (the welfare system administered by the bishop) set up to take care of those needs. You cannot expect the Lord to bless your efforts if you choose to handle problems in a way other than how he has revealed. If you find someone with a genuine need, channel that person to the bishop. You must not leave your ministry to try to magnify the bishop's call to meet the temporal needs of the people. You may face frustrations, because the bishop may not move as quickly as you think he should. Remember, welfare is one of his responsibilities, and he will be inspired to magnify his office the same as you will be inspired to magnify yours.

Learn your financial lessons well. So much time and worry can be saved when missionaries work together to make financial matters contribute to their primary work (saving souls) rather than become a point of conflict between companions.

12

DON'T WAIT FOR OTHERS TO MAKE YOU SUCCESSFUL

SOME TEENAGERS GREW UP expecting someone else to do things for them. For example, if a Sunday School class was boring, it was the teacher's fault. If there was no life at a Church dance, it was someone else's fault. If you weren't having fun living, it was as if someone else was supposed to do something for you. Unfortunately, too many missionaries carry this same childish attitude with them into their missions. However, you must realize that no one can pave the way for you. If you want life to be fun and interesting, you must assume some responsibility. Likewise, if you are not enjoying your mission, take charge of the situation and make appropriate changes.

Your companion may exhibit a rather negative attitude about the mission and life in general. In this situation it is tempting to take a deep breath, roll your eyes, and just wait until transfers. But remember, every day that you allow your companion to smother your enthusiasm is one less day you will serve your mission the way you want. What can you do about his or her negative attitude? Generally, it is difficult to be around an optimistic person and maintain a sullen, depressed attitude. The first thing you can do is to be the kind of missionary you want to be in spite of your companion's sour attitude.

Next, you can reason with your companion and perhaps learn why he or she is that way. The possibilities are endless: low self-esteem, a troubled home, a struggling testimony. Before you write your companion off, try to find out what is wrong.

Depressed people are not happy people, and their lives are miserable. If your companion has been able to identify what is wrong, he or she may not know what to do about it. Be a supportive companion and tactfully give some good practical advice—it may give your companion new hope. It's all too easy for some missionaries to rigidly state, "I'm not here to baby-sit my companion. If he has a problem, then it's his problem." Unfortunately, your companion's problems become your problems. After you have talked through the problem, make some positive plans for overcoming the problem. Don't dwell on the problem—an approach used by too many depressed people. Look for the positive in every situation, though sometimes it is very difficult. When people are depressed, everything seems dark. To them there is no evident way out! If you wait for the mission president to visit with your companion, you may waste a lot of valuable time.

When faced with obstacles seemingly too large to handle, many people choose the easy way out by doing nothing to try to surmount them or by complaining. Neither reaction does any good. No matter what the situation or problem, you have three options: (1) not let it bother you, (2) complain about it and let it affect the quality of your mission, or (3) evaluate the situation and do something about it.

If you choose to do nothing or complain, you stand the chance of ruining your attitude toward your mission. All the adversary has to do is keep you in touch with those who are likewise negative, contrary, or unsupportive. If your life can be controlled simply by keeping the wrong kinds of people around you, your trying to wait out the situation could have very negative eternal implications. If you decide to do something, the very worst you can do is fail, and things will remain the same as before. If you are afraid of hard work, the world will be a pretty bleak place to live. No one is assigned to smooth the way for you. If you want a smooth road, plan on smoothing it out yourself. If you adopt a "can do" attitude, most of the problems become little more than irritations. Over the past three years, I have witnessed astounding results when missionaries decided they didn't like the way things were going and decided to make a difference. Despised companions became best of friends, unsupportive wards became the most desirable places in the mission to serve, and apartments formerly labeled "Outer Darkness" became pleasant abodes. But only you can make the difference.

Sometimes determining that you cannot change things and then not letting them bother you may be the only mature decision. You may wish that the weather was not so cold or hot, dry or wet, windy or calm, or whatever. Unless there is a truly pressing need expedient in the eyes of the Lord, he surely is not going to alter the weather to suit your particular whim. On a more practical note, you may not like the way the mission president chooses leaders in the mission—yet that may be the style of leadership most sensible and comfortable to him. It may not be right or wrong, good or bad, just different. Allowing that difference to sour your attitude will cut you off from spiritual experiences. Choosing leaders is part of his stewardship, so why not be content to magnify your own calling? Try not to become upset when the president magnifies his. When you become a leader, you will want to do things in ways that feel right to you, without having to worry whether every other person agrees with your philosophy.

Be careful in making changes that you believe need to be made. Some things you desire are just a matter of personal preference. Remember that everyone has a right to his or her own personal likes and dislikes. Trying to impose your personal desires on others gives the impression that you are the only one who is important, and that immediately labels you as selfish. Learning the difference between right and wrong and your personal likes and dislikes takes some practice. Learning the balance between being too passive and too aggressive will take time but will be rewarding in the future.

Determining whether things can and ought to be changed is a talent that will bless you forever. There is a time to lead and a time to be led. There is a time to change and a time to leave things alone. There is a time to motivate and solve problems and a time to seek for more experienced help. Happy is the missionary who learns to discern when each of these times are.

13
....

HOMESICKNESS

Some missionaries believe they will never suffer from homesickness. Since it cannot be detected by a thermometer or a doctor, it may go undetected for some time. It is a potentially debilitating condition that should not be taken lightly. Fortunately, it is curable and never fatal.

As you are given opportunities to shoulder the added responsibility of leadership, this chapter may help you diagnose and treat this common ailment. How do you recognize the symptoms of homesickness? It can start in the MTC or may surface later, usually during the first three to five months in the mission field. You may wake up one morning, look at the ceiling, and say to yourself, "I am not cut out to be a missionary! I need to go home! I am wasting my time here!" Or you may occasionally catch yourself thinking about home— on holidays, for instance, and feel pangs of homesickness. Don't worry. Such feelings are a normal and healthy part of your mission.

It is common for an elder or sister who has never been away from family before to experience severe homesickness. Even if you went away to school before your mission, you probably will experience a degree of homesickness. It is comforting to know that almost every missionary experiences homesickness to some extent. Homesickness can drain your desire to get up, to study, to go out proselyting, to eat, or even to enjoy P-day activities. The sooner you recognize what is happening to you or a fellow missionary, the easier it is to put it in perspective and cure it.

Admitting that you are homesick does not make you a wimp or a baby; it is a normal reaction to change. You are closing the door on the only chapter of your life that you have known—your premission chapter. You have been separated from family, friends, and loved ones and have undergone a dramatic change in lifestyle. You were comfortable at home; even if conditions weren't perfect there, you were familiar with people, places, schedules, and activities. But, now you have begun a new chapter that will drastically change your life. You may be overhauling your priorities. Premission things like cars, ball games, goofing off, television, and hanging out may become less important. Personal relationships, spiritual feelings, reading the scriptures, Church meetings, general conferences, families, eternal goals, and temple marriage will likely become primary goals in your life. No wonder there may be the last, longing look back at the old days that causes you to feel confused and homesick. You may be reluctant to let go of the familiar because the chapter you are opening, although exciting and new, is uncharted. Will you be able to survive and succeed? Will your friends back home still accept the new you? Will others view you as a goody-goody? The questions are endless, and the answers may not yet be clear to you.

When you realize what is happening, you will be at a crossroad in your life. You can call it quits or you can grit your teeth, redouble your efforts, and move on. The following chapter will sensitize you to the temptations and problems that the adversary may put in your way as the normal thoughts of going home early cross your mind. If you have firmly determined to serve your full mission whatever the problems, it will be much easier to look for options that will help you enjoy every day of your mission.

What can you do about homesickness? It is relatively simple. You just say to yourself, "This is exactly what I was warned about. Where do I go from here?" Then get out of bed and onto your knees and explain to your Heavenly Father how you feel. Tell him how you want to succeed but need his help to keep things in an eternal perspective. Promise him that you'll do everything in your power if he will help you through this time. Then get up off your knees and go to work.

Start by serving your companion. Polish his shoes, wash the dishes, iron his shirt or her dress, make your companion's bed while he or she is in the shower. Put on a happy face and take control. As you leave the apartment, keep smiling (even though you may not want to). Find someone to serve: a member who needs yard work done, an investigator who is painting a fence, a stranger who needs help roofing, a teacher whose students could use your help in one-on-one tutoring, an older person who just needs someone to talk to, a doctor who could use help with therapy patients. The list is endless. As you begin to lose your life in service, you will find that homesickness disappears and seldom returns. Instead of concentrating on yourself, focus on the needs of others. You will appreciate how many blessings you have and realize how much you can bless others by alleviating their suffering, worries, loneliness, or other challenges. As you forget yourself and remember others, the Lord will answer your humble prayer and help you overcome homesickness.

As you return home exhausted every evening, you will

realize that you've never felt better in your life. As you read the scriptures with real intent, you will receive insight and knowledge like never before. As you lose yourself in the service of others, you will experience true feelings of charity and love. You will realize that many of your teenage activities were shallow and unrewarding compared to these new feelings. As you kneel before your Heavenly Father, your heart will feel full, and often tears of gratitude and love will accompany your realization of the value of your mission experiences.

Hopefully, you will not need the counsel given in this chapter, but if you do, it will be here for you. You may find that other activities help you beat the blues. The cure may be singing a song with your companion, memorizing and quoting scriptures or inspirational quotes or poetry, writing in your journal, or writing to a friend at home or another missionary in another part of the world. Don't be afraid to talk with other missionaries and ask how they overcame homesickness. Sharing ideas and experiences will help them remember how they did it, and this will prepare them to help other missionaries as well.

Does homesickness ever return? Sometimes it does if you have a couple of trying days, receive bad news from home, or serve with a particularly challenging companion. Be particularly mindful that the holiday season between Thanksgiving and New Year's is especially difficult. Other prominent holidays when your family gathers may prove challenging no matter how long you have served. If homesickness comes back, the same prescription that cured you before will work again. I like President Ezra Taft Benson's statement to newly called mission presidents in 1982: "One of the greatest secrets of missionary work is work! If a missionary works, he will get the Spirit; if he gets the Spirit, he will teach by the Spirit; and if he teaches by the Spirit, he will touch the hearts of the people and he will be happy. *There will be no homesickness,* no worrying about families, for all time and talents and interests are centered on the work of the ministry. Work, work, work—there is no satisfactory substitute, especially in missionary work" (*The Teachings of Ezra Taft Benson,* Salt Lake City: Bookcraft, 1988, p. 200, emphasis added).

If you are blessed with no lasting feelings of homesickness, don't despair; you will definitely be tested in other areas. But please be sensitive and have Christlike empathy for those challenged by homesickness.

Whether the homesickness lasts five minutes or five months depends on you. Once you have experienced homesickness yourself, your empathy for other missionaries who are struggling with it will be much greater. Share with them your technique for overcoming homesickness. You become a kind of savior on Mount Zion as you rescue a brother or sister from his or her dark and dreary mental wilderness. You become an instrument in the Lord's hands to guide others out of depression and back into the glorious light of the gospel.

14

....

CALLING HOME

WHEN A MISSIONARY LEAVES home, there are a lot of mixed emotions. Almost everyone has a struggle adjusting to missionary life. Everything familiar is absent. Feelings of loneliness are normal and can be expected. Usually those feelings are overcome by burying yourself in the work.

Some mission rules vary from mission to mission. Those serving in remote and isolated areas may not have the option of calling home, even if the mission president allows it. Those who serve in countries where telephones are available must decide, "Am I willing to obey the mission rule concerning calling home or not?" If you decide to obey it so you can enjoy the fulness of the Spirit and earn the promised rewards for diligent service, some guidelines here may prove helpful.

Don't guess what the mission's rule for calling home is. Other missionaries may have their own interpretation of what the president expects, based on how diligent they are in following his counsel. Ask the mission president yourself. Usually in the initial orientation, either the mission president or his wife will cover the rules of their mission. There will almost always be a time to ask questions. If the calling-home rule is not covered, ask for clarification.

If the policy allows you to call home, find out when you are allowed to call. Our mission designated three calls a year:

Christmas, Mother's Day, and one other discretionary time. If you are allowed to call home on Mother's Day, find out if the rule permits you to phone your father also if your parents are divorced. Usually common sense is the deciding factor. Remember, the mission president is just there to help, not to make you choose between Mom and Dad.

You may wonder why a calling-home policy even exists. We observed that those who broke the rule never really learned how to trust and rely on their Heavenly Father, because the communication lines were still active between them and their earthly parents. The more you are required to seek your Heavenly Father's help in solving difficult problems, the faster your ability to receive answers to prayers will mature. The more you call Mom or Dad for advice, the less you depend on heavenly counsel. From the time you were separated from your mother at birth, you have been developing your ability to exercise free agency. Learn how to stand without your parents' constant direction.

If you are allowed to call home, use common sense. Your budget will not permit lengthy calls. This does not refer to your financial budget (Mom and Dad may have enough money to handle whatever bill you incur), but your time budget. Remember that you committed to serve the Lord with "all your heart, might, mind and strength" and that you would keep your "eye single to the glory of God." If you are honest with yourself, you will discover that a twenty-minute conversation home takes a lot longer than twenty minutes. You may want to plan your call in advance, making a list of what to ask, whom to talk to, and which directions you want to give regarding your return and your future. You may also become anxious about whether your boyfriend or girlfriend will be there to talk with you and how you should talk to her or him with the family standing around.

The phone call will pass rather quickly. For the next week or so, you will recall often what was said. If you sensed problems at home, you may find yourself worrying about how everyone is really doing. You may find that your little brother's voice has changed or your little sister sounds so grown-up. Concerns about fitting back into the family will also crop up. But problems, changes, and concerns are all natural facts of life. Unless you are disciplined and focused on the work, days, weeks, or months may elapse with only a minimal amount of time focused on missionary work. Your time budget cannot afford that.

Some parents may even suggest that you call more often than the rules permit. The most beneficial thing you can do is explain the rules to them and request their assistance in helping you be obedient. Just about the only way they can call you, unless they call the mission office, is if you give them your telephone number. Do yourself a favor—don't send the number home. In the event of an emergency, they can call the mission president, who will either contact you immediately or give them your number.

When you do call home, keep the conversation focused on missionary work. What a wonderful opportunity it is to let them feel the Spirit through your voice and what you talk about. Miracles happen in the families of missionaries who use their phone calls to reinforce and strengthen their families. If you find it a bit uncomfortable talking with your family, use the skills you have learned from the *Missionary Guide* to put them at ease and build on common ground. Usually it is difficult to help them understand that although you love them dearly, you really can't talk all day.

One of the most spiritually destructive phone calls you could make as a missionary would be to your boyfriend or girlfriend. I don't know of any mission president in the world that permits or encourages his missionaries to call "significant others." The effect is devastating. Old romantic feelings are renewed. Satan takes full advantage, encouraging you to daydream, fantasize, and otherwise divert your attention from missionary work. Occasionally, unwise missionaries send their phone numbers home to special friends. They may not realize that these calls will rob them of the Spirit for longer than they can afford to be without it. If you have already made the mistake, write your friend a letter and ask that the number be destroyed and to please not call. Whenever we put our boyfriend or girlfriend before the mission rules, we have actually positioned them before our devotion to God. Following the persuasions of our friends or families rather than the mission rules is a form of idolatry, which is hardly a characteristic of a candidate for the celestial kingdom's highest degree of glory.

It isn't usually the membership-threatening rules that cause the spiritual downfall that some missionaries experience. Little rationalizations begin to grow and increase with time until total disobedience can be readily justified. Either you are obedient or you are not. Eventually there will be no middle ground.

For those who would rather make a tape recording than write letters, stop and reconsider. It usually takes longer to record a tape than to write a letter. It is your P day that you are using, but it is also your companion's P day. The time you spend talking into a microphone will bring fruits less permanent than those resulting from time spent writing a letter. Why? It is rather simple. Two of our daughters served missions while we were on our mission. When they would make an occasional tape, we found that they would try to include their companions or other missionaries in the district or zone. Usually everyone became childishly silly, probably because they were uncomfortable and didn't know what to say or how to react. They talked about objects visible to them at the moment. Their thoughts were not as organized as they would be in a letter. We would only listen to the tape once. On the other hand, we would read their letters over and over. We could use parts of them in talks or zone conferences. We also used them in family home evenings, visits from friends, counseling missionaries, and uplifting ourselves when needed. The difference in the comparative value of tapes and letters was so great that we encouraged them not to send tapes unless there was an imperative reason.

Of course, my counsel on tapes is a personal observation. Making tapes is not against mission rules. But after our personal experience and that of the elders and sisters I have counseled, I believe the counsel is sound. In general, you will keep letters for the rest of your life, but you may never listen to tapes again. Let your communication time with the home front be more lasting than a single experience.

15
....

THE HONEYMOON STAGE OF COMPANIONSHIP

THE FIRST WEEK OR SO OF THE companionship is referred to as "the honeymoon." During this period both companions generally try to impress each other with how righteous and obedient they are. This is a wonderful time to do as the Lord commanded in Doctrine and Covenants 88:119: "Establish a house."

Experience has proven that if companions will sit down the very first night they are together and establish the ground rules, it is much easier to make necessary corrections after the honeymoon.

What kind of rules and procedures should you establish? Start at the beginning of the day and work your way through. For example, you might say, "Elder, let's agree to keep the get-up-on-time rule. If one of us sleeps in a little, how do you suggest we get each other up?" Or you might say, "I prefer that you set the alarm clock by my head and turn on the alarm. How would you like me to get you up?" With approaches like these, you are still in the laughing stage and can generally invent creative ways to wake your sleepy companion.

When I served my first mission in Samoa, I had a

Samoan companion who was a five-foot-tall, 350-pound wall of muscle. He taught me the honeymoon approach. His heart was in the right place, but his head just wouldn't respond to a 6:00 A.M. wake-up call. As we sat in our *fale* (home) that first evening, he said, "Elder Bott, I want to be obedient. You've probably heard horror stories about me sleeping in. You get me up at six o'clock every morning." I wasn't new to the mission field, and I did know of his reputation. I said to him, "Elder Paiali'i, how do you want me to get you up?" He said, "Shake me a little, and if I don't get up, throw a glass of water in my face." (I may be slow, but I was not stupid!) He quickly added, "Then run like heck! I will chase you for about ten steps before I wake up. Don't let me catch you in the first ten steps, or you are history. After ten steps, I'll be awake and you'll be all right." I thought, *This must be a sure ticket to the spirit world.*

At 6:00 A.M., I lifted his mosquito net and shook him gently. He grunted and told me to get lost. I was tempted to follow his directive. But true to the promise I had made the night before, I shook him again more firmly. This time he opened one eye and again ordered that I leave him alone. I shook him a third time, reminding him that cold water would be my next wake-up call. He told me my time on earth would come to an end if I doused him.

After a few minutes of serious pondering, I went for the glass of water. With a prayer in my heart and the pathway out of the *fale* clear, I doused him with the water. For a short, stocky guy, he could really move. He came out from under his sheet on a dead run. I had never been more motivated to move quickly as I tried to stay ahead of him. But true to his word, we had gone about ten steps when he stopped, announced that he was awake, and told me to return. I then had to make a life-determining decision: Was he trying to trick me back so he could finish me off, or was he really awake and ready to go? I slowly inched my way back toward my wet companion, who greeted me with a big Polynesian smile. As I approached him, he reached up to put his arm around my shoulder, but I winced like a disciplined puppy. I thought he would crush me, but he didn't! He was awake and happy. We joked about it during the day as we proselyted. Just before bed, he again charged me to wake him in the morning. The next morning was like a rerun of the previous morning. The second glass of water brought another string of threats, whose fulfillment I trembled to contemplate, as he pursued me toward the beach. Again I returned to find him happy and awake.

The third morning, I told him I was going to douse him again, so he might as well get up on his own. He assured me that he wouldn't be as easy on me this time. My faith almost failed me. I decided that it would be better to fulfill my commitment and die obedient rather than give in to pressure. Again, he shot out of bed when the water hit him, chased me for ten steps, stopped, invited me back and (thankfully) was awake and congenial like before. That was the last morning I had to douse him.

He always considered me his favorite companion, and he definitely was one of mine. I asked him why he liked being with me, and he taught me another lesson. He said, "I knew I should get up on time, but sometimes it's hard to be good without someone to help you."

After watching elders and sisters as a missionary in Samoa and also as a mission president, I am convinced that missionaries really want to do what is right. It is just that sometimes, as the Savior observed, "The spirit indeed is will-ing, but the flesh is weak" (Matthew 26:41).

Always try to motivate your companion to be a good, obedient missionary each day. But don't stop there! Devise a plan to handle a problem if either of you slips a little. If you have decided beforehand, then a kind reminder like "Remember that's what we decided to do" will usually bring things back into perspective. If you decide to try to force obedience on your companion, he or she will probably rebel, and ugly scenes could jeopardize your friendly relationship.

The following are just a few areas that need established game plans: getting up, companionship study, leaving on time, cleaning the apartment (including clothes, dishes, and clutter), length of time at members' homes, what to do when an appointment falls through, what time to be in at night, association with members of the opposite sex, and talking about nonmission topics such as premission activities, post-mission plans, and girlfriends or boyfriends. You will find that the list grows as your experience with other missionaries increases. Toward the end of your mission, it may take three or four hours to establish ground rules. It is worth every minute.

One word of caution: Don't try to force your personal preferences on your companion just because you are senior companion, have been in the area longer, or feel you are more spiritual than your companion. If a rule is in the white handbook or is a directive by your mission president, there is no need to negotiate. However, how you spend the leisure hours of your P day should be established by a more coop-erative approach. You may like sports, while your compan-ion likes museums or historical points of interest. Don't always insist on doing it your way. You may decide to alternate P-day activities, or maybe your companion will accompany you to play sports for a couple of hours (even if he or she reads or studies while you play), and then you can accompany your companion for a couple of hours to his or her choice of activities. Be creative to ensure a win-win environment.

It is never too late to establish the rules. If you forget to do it the first day, do it as soon as you remember. No one enjoys living in an uncomfortable environment. The Spirit cannot dwell amid contention and bickering. It will be a bit more difficult to make rules after the honeymoon, because you will both be aware of the other's weaknesses. Agree to clean the slate and not to dredge up old complaints. Once you have established the rules, be tolerant and forgiving. Habits are difficult to break. In fact, you will not achieve perfection during your mission or after in this lifetime. The Prophet Joseph Smith said, *"When you climb up a ladder, you must begin at the bottom, and ascend step by step, until you arrive at the top; and so it is with the principles of the Gospel— you must begin with the first, and go on until you learn all the principles of exaltation. But it will be a great while after you have passed through the veil before you will have learned them. It is not all* to be comprehended in this world; it will be a great work to learn our salvation *and exaltation even beyond the grave"* (*Teachings of the Prophet Joseph Smith*, p. 348; italics in original).

Modifying lifelong habits can be difficult. Be patient and kind, and others will likely return the same considerations to you. If you choose to ignore a companion's disobedience (or your own), the Spirit will gradually withdraw; you will not enjoy your mission nearly as much as you could if you were willingly obedient. Missionaries do not regret being too obedient. But bitter tears accompany many who, at the end of their missions, regret their irresponsibility and disobedience. Remember, you have only one chance to serve your present mission honorably.

16
....

COMMUNICATION SKILLS

EFFECTIVE COMMUNICATION is the key to successful companionships, working with members, and teaching investigators.
Too often we think that communication is just telling
another person how we feel. Sometimes we say things that
are intended to inform a companion of our feelings, but
instead they only cause more tension. Perhaps a review of
communication principles would help avoid those painful
experiences that leave us feeling like a total failure.

During the first week or so of your companionship
decide on a specific time each week when you and your companion will sit down and evaluate your work. If you establish a time and a place from the very beginning, it will be
easy for one or both of you to remember these meetings,
which are called companionship inventories. It isn't a time to
rip on your companion and point out all his or her faults
and weaknesses. Among other things, it can be a time when
you express your love for each other, congratulating each
other on work well done.

Timing is critical. If you try to hold the inventory when
one of you is tired, hungry, irritable, too hot or cold, or sick
or otherwise uncomfortable, you are destined to fail. Choose
a time when you both feel fresh, relaxed, and talkative. You
might decide to use companionship study time on your

P day to hold the inventory. Be alert enough to recognize when the inventory is starting to deteriorate and should be postponed. But avoid getting in the habit of postponing the session. Sometimes you just have to force yourself to sit and talk things out. Here are some suggestions that can help you make companionship inventories pleasantly productive.

1. Begin the companionship inventory with prayer. Plead for the Spirit to help you express yourselves in a way that would be consistent with the spirit of the gospel. If you have decided during your initial meeting (during the honeymoon stage) that you want to strive for a near-perfect companionship, then you both will look forward to identifying areas in which you are falling short.

2. Make sure your physical positioning is correct. Don't sit opposite each other across the table—the very position suggests confrontation. In fact, you may enjoy the inventories more when you are outside, perhaps sitting or walking in a park or some other pleasant therapeutic surrounding. If you decide to stay in your apartment, sit next to each other on the sofa or at the table. The reason for this is both symbolic and literal. When you identify problems, shoot at them, and miss, you will hit your companion if he or she is sitting opposite you. Remember, you are on the same team. You want to attack the issue, not the companion.

3. Start with the positive. Find something good and encouraging about the way things are going. If you can't make a single positive comment about each other or the work, you are not being honest with each other. Even the most strained companionships have bright spots. If you are getting along fairly well, most of your inventory could be spent in reviewing the highlights of your companionship. Be honest. Lack of sincerity is easily detected and damages relationships more than almost anything else.

4. Select two or three areas in which you want to improve. If you identify *all* of the areas that need improvement, you may both feel overwhelmed. In identifying the problem, be careful to identify the problem itself—don't attack your companion. Don't say, "You are a slob! You always leave dirty clothes around the apartment." You might rephrase your observation to say something like, "I feel the Spirit more strongly when our apartment is clean. How can we help each other take care of the dirty clothes?" The message is clear without a pointing finger of condemnation. Other situations require another subtle approach. If you have noticed that your companion often seems to lose interest during your part of the discussion, you might approach him by saying, "Elder, when you do not appear attentive during the discussion, our investigators think you are not interested in what is going on. Is there something wrong?" Like it or not, right or wrong, your companion must deal with your well-intentioned perception—and you must deal with his, too. Perhaps there's an innocent explanation: he hasn't been able to sleep because his girlfriend is marrying someone else. It might be a serious situation: he has health problems that he is reluctant to talk about.

5. After identifying the problems, immediately start working on solutions. Don't be content to come up with a single possible solution unless the solution is obvious. For instance, in the example of leaving the dirty clothes around, one solution might be to have an inspection call just before mealtime. Everyone in the apartment puts away everything that is out of place. A second option might be that one companion cooks breakfast while the other cleans up the apartment. A third solution might be a twenty-five-cent fine for leaving clothes in piles. The money could be kept in a jar and used for treats at the end of the week. A fourth solution might be a laundry bag set up in a corner of the room. Each basket counts two points as dirty clothes (except garments) are wadded into a ball and shot free-throw style into the basket. The high scorer for the week wins a free dinner from the other missionaries in the apartment. A fifth solution could be an appointed policeman who gathers up all dirty clothes left out. At the end of the week, the offending missionaries have to buy back their clothes so they can do their laundry. You may think I have labored the point, but my intent is to show you that with a little creativity, most, if not all, problems have more than one possible solution. Keeping the apartment clean won't be drudgery if you make it a game.

6. *Agree on definite plans of action for each problem and establish a means of accountability.* If there is no accountability, your decisions will be forgotten and progress will not be made. For example, continue to check up on each other's progress in targeted areas during your companionship inventories. Give and receive reports. Praise, apologize, recommit. If it is appropriate to the nature of the problem, hold each other accountable to report nightly on progress made toward your individual and mutual goals and plans.

7. *Be flexible if perfection isn't achieved overnight.* It is difficult to change from Mr. Slob to Mr. Clean in one day. There will be some setbacks, but they will become less frequent as you follow through with your decisions. Be kind and considerate of your apartment mates. They may have been raised differently, so be reasonable! Don't try to impose a standard on others that no one is willing or able to achieve.

The next part of avoiding miscommunications is so

obvious that many overlook it. If you want to know what your companion is thinking, *ask*. After you have served together for a number of weeks or months, you begin to believe that you know what he or she is thinking. This is when problems begin in companionships (as in marriages). You and your companion do not think exactly alike. Perhaps my wife will pardon one example that illustrates that point. Every night, schedules permitting, we would go for a walk around the subdivision where the mission home was located. We would hold our companionship inventories during those walks and discuss problems facing the mission. We never lacked topics to talk about. The course was a little more than one and a half miles long. If we were having a challenging day, we would walk twice around the course. One particular day we were on our fourth trip around the course. As we walked, enjoying the warm, moonlit summer night, Sister Bott became silent. I immediately reviewed in my mind what I had said that could have upset her. I couldn't identify anything. As the adversary tempts us to do, I started thinking of all the possible reasons for her silence. Finally, I decided to apply the principle of "ask if you want to know." I asked, and her answer taught me a great lesson. She said, "Have you noticed how the moonlight through those trees casts a shadow on the road that looks like venetian blinds?" I could never have guessed that she was pondering moonlight and shadows. We've often laughed about that statement, but the lesson is one that, if applied, could save countless arguments in the mission (and in marriage)—if you want to know something, *ask!*

A word of caution. There may be times when you or your companion is just in a bad mood. This is not a good time to talk. It seems advisable to have a sign to warn that it would be better to postpone any problem-solving sessions. We suggested that our missionaries use the athletic time-out signal (a "T" made by holding one hand horizontal, palm down, with the other hand vertical under and touching the palm of the horizontal hand). This sign means: "I'm upset. Leave me alone. I'm having a difficult time controlling myself. If I'm forced to talk, I might just lose control. Let me work it out for an hour or so, and I'll be back to talk things out later." If you use this sign, immediately start praying, talk yourself out of your mental state, and get ready to work out the problems so the work is not interrupted. If your companion gives you the time-out sign, immediately start trying to figure out what you have done wrong that has caused the problem. It shouldn't be too difficult to identify the problem. Then, in the spirit of humility and prayer, try to find possible solutions before he or she returns to talk things out.

Other times, you may be in a sober mood, thinking about the scriptures, life, gospel doctrine, family, or whatever. You are not mad, but just need some time alone with your thoughts. When your companion approaches you because you are so quiet, you may want to have a different sign. Since you aren't really mad, the time-out signal would send the wrong message. We use a tug on the right earlobe, which means: "I'm not mad. I'm just thinking. I need a little time by myself without interruption. Give me awhile, and if it is appropriate, I'll share what I'm thinking about." This sign sends an entirely different message than the time-out signal.

Be honest in using these signals. If you are angry, don't tug on your earlobe. If you are not angry, don't give the time-out signal. Because you are required to be with your companion twenty-four hours a day, seven days a week, your companion has a better chance to react in an acceptable manner to you if he or she understands your thoughts or your mood. A companion who is unwilling to communicate is a pain to everyone. Many mission presidents won't let missionaries sulk or remain silent for long periods of time. Certainly sulking is not a Godlike attribute. You must learn to control those feelings sooner or later, so why not sooner?

17
......

"ATTITUDE DETERMINES ALTITUDE"

IS THERE SUCH A THING AS AN easy mission or a hard mission? Every mission in the world presents its own challenges. My first mission in Samoa was a physically difficult but socially easy mission. The wonderful Polynesian people invited us into their homes and shared with us their last morsel. We were never denied entrance into their homes—a stark contrast to many missions in the world! I served for ten of the thirty months under famine conditions brought on by three major hurricanes. It was a physically tough mission.

Only you can determine how tough your mission will be. As a mission president, I remember hearing missionaries complain that they only got five DAs (dinner appointments) a week, while other missionaries were grateful if they had one or two. Some missionaries complained because they had to eat a certain dish more than once a week, while others humbly ate whatever was served.

If you enter the mission with the attitude that people are supposed to serve you, it will be a long eighteen months or two years. On the other hand, if you go to serve and teach, you will be humbly grateful for anything and everything people do for you. It would be wonderful if all members were missionary-minded and had unlimited funds to satisfy the physical wants of missionaries. Unfortunately, many members are still developing their abilities to apply the gospel. Equally as unfortunate from our perspective is the severity of life's trials—many Saints are barely surviving financially. In that case, anything they do for you is a great personal sacrifice.

I remember that during a famine in Samoa people would give us the fish head to eat. This part symbolized respect and was given because of their high esteem for us. Before I understood their reasoning, I complained to my companion that I would like a little less respect and a lot more fish. How selfish I was.

As you are invited into the homes of members and non-members for dinners, remember to write a thank-you note on the back of one of your name cards. Leave it in an inconspicuous place where they will find it after you are gone. You are much more likely to be invited back again if you express your appreciation. What do you write? It doesn't have to be lengthy, profound, or intellectual, but it must be sincere. "Thank you for a wonderful meal and great company. You will certainly be mentioned in our journals tonight. Love, Elders Smith and Brown." Or "You are so thoughtful to share your family dinner hour with us. May the Lord bless you abundantly because of your Christlike charity. Love, Sisters Jones and Anderson." You can think of a thousand short notes that express your appreciation. Reading the Topical Guide entries on service, gratitude, and thankfulness might also help you.

You can and must control your attitude. Too many missionaries wait around complaining because somebody needs to do something for them. What a destructive attitude. If you really want a helping hand you can rely on in every time of need, look on the end of your own arm. On the far end of our mission was a little town that was either "feast or famine." Missionary after missionary went there and all pleaded in their letter to the president that he close the town and pull out the missionaries. Finally, two optimistic elders were sent there with the express charge to "find the Lord's elect" (see D&C 29:7). They were told that although it would be tough at first, the Saints who lived there were wonderful. The elders believed it and went to work. For the first month, it was tough going. People were reluctant to trust these missionaries because previous missionaries had not built up a strong relationship with them.

These creative elders started putting little thoughts or scriptures in the hymn books on the page of the opening song. Eyebrows were raised, smiles exchanged, and hearts softened. Support for the missionaries soon followed. In the second month there were five baptisms. Within the following three months, twenty-five people were baptized. That town became the most desirable place to serve in the entire mission. What made the difference? The attitude of the missionaries.

Whoever said, "If you think you can or you can't, you're right" was right on target. It may not be easy to keep a positive attitude when everything seems to be going wrong, but it is possible. The day I arrived in Samoa, I was met by a little missionary named Filipo. He must have noticed us drooping in the 98° F temperature with humidity to match. The leis around our necks only added to our discomfort. He grabbed me by the shirt and said, "Elder Bott, I challenge you never to spend a discouraged day in Samoa." I looked down at him and thought, *If he can, I can.* Little did I know then that I would spend ten months living on coconuts and raw fish, or have yellow jaundice, or be marooned on a hostile island—a situation requiring the mission president to request that the U.S. Coast Guard rescue us. I didn't know then that I would have a tropical ulcer that would threaten the amputation of my foot, or that I would suffer from salt hunger to the point that I would drink sea water and lick the perspiration off my arms in an attempt to satisfy that hunger. If I could have found Filipo, I'd have taken back my promise. But I decided to be true to my word. I can truthfully say that I never had an entirely discouraging day for thirty months in Samoa, nor have I in the twenty-six years since then. I will be eternally grateful for Filipo.

Some days will indeed be tough. However, when you are discouraged, you can't help yourself, your companion, the work, the members, or the Lord. In order to get on the right track, stop where you are and figure out how to rebound. In the islands, it was dressing in our lava lavas and running at top speed up and down the beach until we were exhausted, then lying down and watching the seagulls take pot shots at us. Physical exercise always seemed to help us put things in better perspective.

You must know yourself well enough to know what can bring you out of a slump. These ten suggestions might help you deal with discouragement.

1. The earlier you can recognize that you are slipping, the easier it is to stop.

2. It helps to have a plan to refresh your outlook. Maybe there is someone whose need, whether greater than yours or not, will help you to lose yourself in service, thereby allowing the Spirit to displace your discouragement and rekindle your enthusiasm.

3. Avoid negative self-talk, one of the most self-defeating habits we engage in. When we wallow in self-pity, telling ourselves how bad we have it, we feed upon the psychological elements that cause depression and discouragement. You may think, *No one has it as bad as I do* or, *I have a right to be discouraged.* Even if those thoughts were true, it serves no useful purpose to entertain them. Force yourself to look on the bright side.

4. Serving others can also help.

5. Find a "sacred grove" where you and your companion can retreat for a moment of prayer, scripture reading, and meditation, to ponder or just plain relax.

6. In almost any setting, depression will fade if you will "count your many blessings, [naming] them one by one" (*Hymns,* 1985, no. 241). You will rapidly gain an overwhelming sense of appreciation for how much God has blessed you.

7. Reread your patriarchal blessing. Pray before you read, asking your Heavenly Father to help you see the advice you need. Often, timely counsel will be given that will help you through the tough times.

8. Write a positive letter to a friend at home or in another mission, giving him or her the much-needed encouragement. It is impossible for you to lift others up if you are not standing on solid ground yourself. Very often, the encouraging counsel you give others will help you find the solutions to your own problems.

9. If you can't cheer up on your own, ask your companion or other trusted Melchizedek Priesthood bearer to give you a blessing. Listen carefully to the words of the blessing and feel the closeness of the Lord.

10. If everything else fails and you can't shake the feelings of depression and discouragement within several days (never

longer than a week), call your mission president for additional help and advice.

Very few missionaries will have to call when they follow these suggestions. You may have others that really work for you to add to this list.

If you work with a companion who tends to look at the negative side, you may have to help train him or her. You will soon learn that negativism and constant complaining quickly drag your spirits down. It is not easy to train a person to look for the good in everything.

A number of years ago, I taught an institute class at Duke University in Durham, North Carolina. Adjacent to the divinity school where I taught is a beautiful Gothic chapel. Its floors are covered with slate so that even the sound of a pin dropped on the floor would echo through the building. The chapel is built in the shape of a huge cross, the ceiling is probably sixty feet high, and each wall is adorned with beautiful stained-glass windows depicting scenes from the Old and New Testaments. Each week before teaching the class, I would go there and sit for an hour or more admiring the windows. As visitors would enter the building, they would instinctively cease talking and marvel at the beauty of the chapel.

One day as I studied the window depicting Adam and Eve, an elderly couple came in rather noisily. As they gazed at the same window I was looking at, the woman said obnoxiously, "Look at that hole in the lower left-hand corner of the window!" Until that very moment, I hadn't noticed it. The couple moved on, but the negativism lingered. Every time I went to the chapel, I always looked for the hole. I was tempted to borrow a ladder, climb up and stick a wad of bubble gum in the hole to block the light from shining through. Surely the gum would have gone unnoticed, and I would again be able to enjoy the glory of the window.

So it is with our lives. If we really look, we can find fault in everything. The Sadducees and Pharisees found fault in Christ, even though there wasn't any fault in him. You may be tempted to look at your local leaders and find fault in them. Don't. You may be inclined to compare members in another area to those where you now serve. Don't. You may have a district leader or a zone leader who is still struggling to learn correct leadership skills. It would be so easy to point out the flaws in his approach or personality. Don't. Remember, you will be judged with the same judgment that you use. I can afford to be very liberal in my praise and very stingy in my criticism, since I will need all the mercy I can get from my Heavenly Father.

How do you handle a companion who has developed a critical attitude? Make a pact with each other during your first week together that you will concentrate on the good in everything. Remind each other when you slip. Reward yourselves when you succeed. Solicit the help of other missionaries, members, and leaders. Once you break the negative habits, you will be able to achieve anything by using your positive attitude.

If your companion does not want to participate, it will be more difficult to do it alone—but it is not impossible. Once he or she sees the benefits of your positive attitude, your companion will likely reconsider and join you. You will not be able to change the whole world from negative to positive, but you will make a difference.

18

LEADERSHIP: DON'T LET IT
GO TO YOUR HEAD

ONE OF THE TRULY INSPIRED programs of the mission is leadership. Unfortunately, for some it is also the most challenging area if either they are so timid that leadership scares them to death or are so confident that others view them as arrogant.

After I had called one young man to be a district leader, he immediately called an investigator and announced over the phone, "Now I'm the Big Cheese around here!" This statement represents the exact opposite of leadership. The Savior gave one small verse that forever silences the debate on what constitutes greatness in leadership: "But he that is greatest among you shall be your servant" (Matthew 23:11).

Perhaps a more accurate way of describing the job of a leader would be "servant leadership." When a leader really gets the vision of the calling, there comes a change in the style of leadership that makes others naturally want to follow. There are (and probably always will be) those who aspire to leadership positions because they want to be seen of men, sit and stand up front, give the talks, receive the glory. A true leader enters the leadership arena knowing that his or her needs will sometimes be the last to be met.

Your first task as a newly called leader is to acquaint yourself with those you serve. Remember, a steward is not the owner, but works under the direction of the owner in controlling resources and personnel. How do you get to know those you will serve? It will never happen until you associate and spend time with them. It may be difficult to get together if your mission is large. Phone calls, district or zone P-day activities, district and zone development meetings, and zone conferences all provide opportunities to observe and associate with your fellow missionaries. Your mission president may have a program of "team-ups" during which you proselyte with another set of elders for a day. As a leader, you will need those days to help you earn another person's trust as well as get to know each missionary's strengths and weaknesses. Almost anyone can put on a facade for a couple of hours, but not for the entire day. Hopefully, before you leave for your own area that night or the next morning, you will have a better idea of what their companionship is really like.

Once you get to know the other missionaries, try to find ways to bless their lives. As a leader, your objective is to help them to be more successful. Determining what and how to teach your district or zone may require endless hours of study, meditation, and prayer. Rather than struggle on your own to become "the Big Cheese," be humble and let the Lord inspire you and mold you into a true leader.

Another vital lesson you will learn is that you can't lead from the rear! You must set the example in every aspect of your missionary life. Prepare to be analyzed and criticized (even misunderstood and condemned) in some things you do. The more closely you live the mission rules and fulfill what is expected of the ideal missionary, the easier it will be to lead by example. Don't allow criticism to get you down or convince you to quit trying.

There are three phases in dealing with criticism. First, ask yourself if the criticism against you is true. Be honest! If you flaunt your position or authority as a leader, then you need to change. Some of the most valuable and most painful mission experiences may come from a new missionary's observation of your attitude or behavior. Be humble enough to accept criticism from anyone. If you believe that the only person who can correct you is the mission president, you drastically limit opportunities for improvement. The president can only see you on rare occasions. If the criticism has grounds, change. Remember to thank the person who offers a suggestion. Don't worry about whether the person's motives are sincere or whether he or she is living better than you. Since our goal is to become like our Savior and our Heavenly Father, we should glory in constructive criticism. Positive feedback will help you identify and overcome those things that impede your progress.

Second, in listening to the criticism, you may discover that the analysis is way off target. Instead of getting angry or reproving, you might profit by stopping and asking yourself, "What am I doing or saying that gives this mistaken impression?" See if you can identify some unconscious gesture or action you are using that sends the wrong message. One of my assistants was a tall, handsome, athletic young man, very self-confident in front of a group. He was well prepared and very competent as a speaker and leader. Not too long after our first round of zone conferences, a number of elders and sisters complained in their letters to me that this assistant seemed conceited. I chose not to protect him from the comments. He was crestfallen when he learned of the criticism.

He wanted to know if he should let someone else serve as assistant to the president. What a humble approach to the problem! We talked seriously in an effort to try to identify the problem. The only thing we could think of was that he had a good physique, was handsome, and was confident when he spoke.

At this point you might be inclined to say, "If the missionaries have a problem with him, that is their problem." Not so. We are called to bring people to Christ, not to drive them away. Together my assistant and I determined that the criticism was without grounds, since he was a humble and faithful elder. We decided on a simple tactic to disarm those who were looking for fault. When he stood at the next zone conference, he was to clear his throat, shuffle his papers a little, and glance quickly from one part of the room to the other—all symptoms of nervousness in a speaker. Then he was to give his talk without any other changes. The response was exactly what we had expected. Those who had been so harsh in their criticism wrote in their next letter how humble he had become. Each in turn pledged their support to this "servant-leader." What had changed? Only their perception of what they thought he was thinking. By the time he returned home, he was one of our most powerful missionaries.

Third, if the criticism is unfounded and you can't think of a way to change the mistaken perception, then you must develop a thicker skin and ignore it. Until the Millennium begins, there will always be people who will be offended when no offense is intended. As a missionary, you will often hear people tell you to "go home and get a real job." Criticisms of your character, family, beliefs, intelligence, looks, and anything else they can think of will be more abundant than you want. Do not antagonize the critic, but also do not hold back from fulfilling your calling.

When other missionaries recognize your sincere desire to bless their lives, your task as a leader will be greatly simplified. They will begin to support you and try to make you look good. Because you are trying to help them be successful, they will want *you* to be successful. Truly, it is a "cast your bread on the water" situation. Your positive messages of needed encouragement will always return to bless you many times over.

Identify someone in the mission who you think is a real leader. Try to discover what makes him or her great. It may be a bishop or stake president, a Relief Society president, or a stake Young Women leader in an area in which you serve. It may be a ward mission leader or an elders quorum president with whom you have worked closely. It may be someone in business or politics whom you have observed. Don't limit your search simply to other missionaries, although your example may indeed come from that group. Try incorporating into your character those leadership qualities that you most admire in your heroes. If a trait is difficult to master, try some refining. Don't be afraid to ask for feedback from your companion, apartment mates, or others who observe you daily. Be thick-skinned enough not to take offense at their comments yet teachable enough to try some of their suggestions.

One of the most difficult facts of leadership is that you can never please everybody all the time. If you try too hard to be a "people pleaser," you will become frustrated, discouraged, and ready to resign. Remember, leadership in the Church is not based on democracy. You can and should solicit input from those who will be influenced by your decisions, but the final decisions are yours. Generally speaking, when people feel they have had a chance to express their ideas and they know the leader has considered their input, they are more willing to support the leader's decision—even if it isn't what they suggested. The dictator's use of force only results in resistance and rebellion. Take a few minutes and reread Doctrine and Covenants 121:34–46, inserting "leader" in the appropriate places. This scripture teaches one of the greatest lessons on leadership you can possibly learn. Control, dominion, or compulsion are forbidden. Attaining qualities such as persuasion, long-suffering, gentleness, meekness, love unfeigned, kindness, pure knowledge, charity, and virtue and shunning hypocrisy and guile should be the goals of a good leader. Remember, however, that being called by the mission president to lead means that you are accountable. If something goes wrong, you must answer for it.

There are only a limited number of leadership positions in the mission. Not everyone who is qualified to be an assistant or zone leader will have the opportunity. You can be totally successful as a missionary without ever serving as a leader—look at the sisters! If you are called to serve, give it your best shot. Learn all you can as a servant-leader. Then when the mission president releases you so some other elder can have an opportunity, step down graciously and do not take it personally. Put yourself in the mission president's shoes. It isn't easy to call every qualified missionary to a leadership position, especially if those being released sulk and complain. You are a leader whether or not you are given a position. Too many missionaries fail to realize that just serving a mission is a leadership role. Setting a good or bad example will lead people to choose and act accordingly.

Some people aspire to certain offices even though they may be the least qualified for the position. Whether they are called or not is really not your concern. The mission president is responsible for calling young men to fill positions. Let him magnify his own office. If you know something about a missionary that would morally disqualify him from serving, it is your responsibility to inform the mission president. However, if he still chooses to call the elder, you have done everything required of you. So sustain the elder and make him look as good as you can. Your support should never be based on whether you like a person; the Lord has called that missionary to serve. Also, the president will never know whether he can count on your support if you pick and choose whom you will sustain.

Leadership is difficult but rewarding. Lessons learned from serving in leadership positions in your mission will help you be more effective for the rest of your life. Allow the Lord to mold you into the person he knows you must be to fulfill those positions to which he has foreordained you.

THE THREEFOLD RECORD
OF YOUR MISSION

YOU ARE PROBABLY LIKE MANY other missionaries who have looked forward to serving a mission with great anticipation. You have often heard from returned missionaries comments like, "That was the greatest two years of my life." You may think you could never forget some of your mission experiences. However, you are human, and time will dull even the sharpest memory. How do you preserve a record of your mission?

Every week you are required to write two letters, the first to the mission president, the second to your parents. What is a president's letter? It is a weekly opportunity to report on your stewardship to your presiding priesthood leader. At the beginning of your mission, you might ask the president if he eventually returns the letters to the missionaries who wrote them. If he does not, you have two options: make a photocopy of your letters before you send them, or ask if his personal secretary would file your letters and return them at the end of your mission. I suspect that most presidents would return them.

What kind of a report do you make to the mission president? Some missionaries just write to fill up the space. Others give a detailed account of how they are doing, what the relationship is with their companion, how supportive local members and priesthood leaders are, and how the work is progressing with investigators. Responding to all of these situations will take several minutes or more, but the time is well worth your effort. Some missionaries decide not to write at all, saying that the president never writes back. Don't be silly! The president receives more than two hundred letters every week—this in addition to the various other problems he must face. You should not expect him to respond to each letter. But this certainly does not mean he doesn't read your letters.

I remember when one elder wrote in the middle of his letter that he didn't think I would really read his letter. I called him on the phone to ask why he thought I wouldn't read it. He was very surprised and flattered that the mission president would read his letter. Another missionary, not believing that I read every letter, quoted part of a nursery rhyme in the middle of his letter. When I called him and read it to him over the phone, he was embarrassed. He vowed not to waste any more of my time with nonsense, and he didn't. Many missionaries would seek advice and ask questions in their letters. I tried to respond to their concerns during the week as my schedule would permit.

If you are faithful in your writing, you will have a week-by-week record of your entire mission, a stewardship report that you could give to the Savior. Make your letters worthwhile, rather than just space fillers. On the more mundane level, write so that the president can read it without using the Urim and Thummim! Although you may be in a hurry or your penmanship isn't that great, take a little extra time to write legibly. One young man had such poor handwriting that I would always read his letter last. Then I would call him on the phone and ask him to tell me what he had said. He would laugh and then rehearse the letter's content. After he had explained what he had written, I would go back and try to read the letter. But rarely could I decipher the scribbling.

The second required letter goes to your family. Too many missionaries come from homes that have suffered a painful divorce. Write to both parents, although you may not like the parent who has moved out. For your parents' benefit as well as yours, write to them both.

The record to your family should be a record of your high points, spiritual experiences, and lessons learned. Some parents want to know everything going on in their missionary's life. You must decide what to share. After three years of experience with more than six hundred elders and sisters writing home, I have learned one thing: if you write a graphic description of your more dangerous situations, the mission president will probably get a phone call from your parents. In fact, one concerned mother wanted to know if she should visit her son, who had been threatened at knife-point by a gang member. I assured her that I had talked with her son and that he was fine. Incidentally, this threatening incident occurred only once during the full two years he served.

I am not suggesting that you lie to your parents or even that you shouldn't tell them the whole truth. It would be wise to report what you are going through in a calm and positive manner. One of our good friends had a son in a rather tough mission. He wrote home from his hospital bed in a matter-of-fact manner that he would be released before the letter arrived home and that the stitches from the knife wound were holding well. This was the only communication the parents had about the incident. A call to the mission president assured them that he was all right and that they shouldn't worry too much.

As you write home to express your love for your family and share missionary experiences, you will have a profound effect on your younger brothers and sisters. Those who may be wavering in their commitment to serve a mission will be strengthened as they see you change, grow, and develop into a real son or daughter of God. Be careful what you write. Your letters will likely be the focal point of conversations more often than you would ever imagine, and moms love to read missionary letters in Relief Society and sacrament meetings. The Lord blesses the letters sent home from the mission field. You probably won't even be chastised for poor penmanship. But again, you should write as neatly as you can; remember, if your family keeps your letters (which you should ask them to do), you will want to read them yourself someday.

Some missionaries have found it helpful to take a supply of journal paper and write their letters home on that. If you take a matching journal for the third record of your mission, you will have a matching set when you get home. Be sure to date each letter and write only what you want your children and grandchildren to read. If you write to your boyfriend or girlfriend, ask him or her to save your letters for you.

As mentioned, the third record of your mission is your journal. Here is where you write to yourself about your progress. In years to come, these personal records will show your children what a mission is and how to prepare properly. Write in your journal about your difficult, frightening, and successful experiences.

Also, write the things of the Spirit, such as impressions,

dreams, insights, or spiritual experiences. You can even bring your journal to general conferences or stake conferences and take notes. Many of our missionaries recorded their impressions and the doctrine we discussed at zone conferences. Since paper is cheap, it is better to write too much rather than not enough. As I look back on my first mission, I wish I had written more. Those things that I did record are priceless. But those feelings and experiences that I thought I would never forget but did not write are gone.

Should you keep a daily diary? That is up to you. Many missionaries found that it was too time-consuming to write every night. Others faithfully set aside fifteen minutes every night to record what had happened during the day. Write in your journal at least once a week. If you wait longer than a week, you will forget important details, emotions, and the spirit of the events. If I had to do it all over again, I would try to write daily.

For those who have girlfriends or boyfriends waiting, be careful about writing romantic feelings in your missionary journal. If you do decide to write about them, record it in your new language (if you are learning a language). Then most people who want to read your journal will not be able to understand what you wrote, unless you choose to translate for them. Remember that the scriptures are our best example of keeping appropriate personal records, and romantic entries there are minimal. Although the Song of Solomon is considered romantic in nature, the Prophet Joseph Smith wrote as he retranslated the Bible: "The Songs of Solomon are not inspired writings" (see footnote at the beginning of the Song of Solomon in the LDS edition of the Bible).

When you put all three records of your mission together,

the so-called best eighteen months or two years of your life will be preserved in writing. President Spencer W. Kimball suggested that even the angels will quote from them. What a powerful record for you, your family, and your friends. Don't shortchange yourself by not maintaining a personal record of your mission.

Two Reasons Why the Spirit Withdraws

YOU ARE SERVING WITH ALL your heart, might, mind, and strength, and then suddenly the Spirit is gone. What is the matter? Is the Lord displeased with you? Should you pack up and go home? Should you call the mission president? Perhaps understanding why the Spirit withdraws from people will help calm your fears. Most of us are aware that when we sin, the Lord gives us a "wake-up call" by withdrawing his Spirit. Isaiah talked about this problem when he taught, "Your iniquities have separated between you and your God, and your sins have hid his face from you, that he will not hear" (Isaiah 59:2). The Lord doesn't expect us to be perfect before he allows us to enjoy his Spirit. But he does expect us to live a certain standard of righteousness according to our level of light and knowledge.

Knowing that every person comes from a different background and has had different opportunities to receive spiritual instruction, the Lord wisely counseled, "Leave judgment alone with me" (D&C 82:23). In theory, the Spirit could leave you because you, knowing better, did something wrong, while it may remain with your companion, even though he participated (perhaps quite innocently) in the same act. That is, it is not your place to pass judgment on whether your companion is qualified to have the Spirit with him or her; for all you know, he or she could be doing rather well considering his or her depth of understanding, experience, and maturity. You should concentrate on *your* constant worthiness.

When the Spirit withdraws, stop and ask yourself, "Am I doing anything wrong now that I wasn't doing an hour ago?" If you are, it will be pretty evident. Then immediately repent, pray for forgiveness, and continue working. You will make mistakes on your mission. One of the great repentance lessons was taught by President Brigham Young, who said, "I do not recollect that I have seen five minutes since I was baptized that I have not been ready to preach a funeral sermon, lay hands on the sick, or to pray in private or in public." How would you like to be able to say that? Thankfully, President Young taught us his method: "I will tell you the secret of this. In all your business transactions, words, and communications, if you commit an overt act, repent of that immediately, and call upon God to deliver you from evil and give you the light of His spirit. Never do a thing that your conscience, and the light within you, tell you is wrong" (in *Journal of Discourses,* 12:103).

Can't you do the same thing? Stop immediately and say, "Heavenly Father, I'm sorry I've made a mistake. I'll try never to do it again; please apply the atoning blood of the Savior in my behalf. If there is anything you want me to do to make it right, reveal it to me, and I'll do it. Otherwise, I will consider the matter closed and go on." Too often we punish ourselves forever because "the spirit indeed is willing, but the flesh is weak" (Matthew 26:41). Our Heavenly Father knows and understands that missionaries are prime targets for the devil and his angels. Although the Lord does not look on sin with the least degree of allowance, he does make allowances for the sinner.

You will discover that life (not just your mission) will require constant repentance as the Lord refines you. You may also discover that some things you previously considered to be "okay" are now wrong.

This realization brings us to the second reason why the Spirit may seem to leave a person. When you master trials and lessons on one level, the Lord may withdraw to some degree the direction of his Spirit, much as a wise parent lets go of a child's hand when the child is wise enough to cross the street without help. You wonder what is wrong. But sensing that you aren't doing anything different than you were an hour ago when you felt the Spirit striving with you, an appropriate response might be to humbly pray and thank your Heavenly Father for having confidence in your ability to move to a higher level of commitment and spirituality. You can then examine your personality, attitude, habits, ways of interacting with people, and your relationship with Deity. If you need to work on an area, the Spirit will let you know. As you consciously work on improving in that area, the Spirit will return.

Time passes, and you will feel fairly confident that you have mastered the new Christlike characteristic. Then the Spirit withdraws. When the Spirit withdraws, you may not feel like being good. But you know you are on the right track, so you bridge the spiritual gap and do what you know you should. Before long, the test is over and the Spirit returns, carrying you to a higher level. This process may seem overly simple, but it accurately describes how the missionaries report their progress. The scriptures also confirm this process. In 2 Chronicles 32:31 is recorded this timely explanation: "God left him, to try him, that he might know all that was in his heart." We must learn to know ourselves well enough so that we are willing to do whatever the Lord requires of us—even when we are not highly motivated by the Spirit to do it.

If you were always in touch with the Spirit, you would not be tempted. President Brigham Young taught this principle in a powerful sermon:

> I ask, is there a reason for men and women being exposed more constantly and more powerfully, to the power of the enemy, by having visions than by not having them? There is and it is simply this—God never bestows upon His people, or upon an individual, superior blessings without a severe trial to prove them, to prove that individual, or that people, to see whether they will keep their covenants with Him, and keep in remembrance what He has shown them. Then the greater the vision, the greater the display of the power of the enemy. And when such individuals are off their guard they are left to themselves, as Jesus was. For this express purpose the Father withdrew His spirit from His Son, at the time he was to be crucified. Jesus had been with his Father, talked with Him, dwelt in His bosom, and knew all about heaven, about making the earth, about the transgression of man, and what would redeem the people, and that he was the character who was to redeem the sons of earth, and the earth itself from all sin that had come upon it. The light, knowledge, power, and glory with which he was clothed were far above, or exceeded that of all others who had been upon the earth after the fall, consequently at the very moment, at the hour when the crisis came for him to offer up his life, the Father withdrew Himself, withdrew

His Spirit, and cast a vail [sic] over him. That is what made him sweat blood. If he had had the power of God upon him, he would not have sweat blood; but all was withdrawn from him and a veil was cast over him, and he then plead with the Father not to forsake him. "No," says the Father, "you must have your trials, as well as others."

So when individuals are blessed with visions, revelations, and great manifestations, look out, then the devil is nigh you, and you will be tempted in proportion to the vision, revelation, or manifestation you have received. Hence thousands, when they are off their guard, give way to the severe temptations which come upon them, and behold they are gone (in *Journal of Discourses*, 3:205–6).

Perhaps you may feel like a Mormon yo-yo! You rise to a certain level, the Spirit withdraws so you can be tempted; you fall back where you were, the Spirit returns to pick you up; then it leaves again and you fall, only to start the process all over again. Wouldn't it be more productive to replace that scenario with one like this: You rise to a certain level, the Spirit leaves so you can be tested; you live the principle you just learned, even though you don't feel particularly motivated to be good; the Spirit returns to help you move to the next higher level; the cycle repeats over and over as the Lord perfects you? Understanding the Lord's process of perfecting you will help you avoid condemning yourself when the Spirit withdraws.

When the Spirit withdraws because of sin, it is like a swift kick in the pants. When the Spirit leaves because you are being tested at a higher level, it is a pat on the back. This congratulatory signal shows that your Heavenly Father is confident that you are ready for the next level in your spiritual progression. It is imperative not to mistake the pat on the back for the kick in the pants. It is equally imperative that you not think you are being congratulated when, in reality, you are being chastised.

The adversary will constantly tell you that the Spirit withdraws because you are bad, have sinned, or are hopelessly lost. Satan wants you to give up and go home disgraced. However, if you know what is really happening to you, you can command him to leave. He is the destroyer, the great deceiver, the eternal pessimist. There is a simple yet effective way to decide if it is Satan telling you that you are worthless or if it is the Lord urging you to move ahead. When the Spirit withdraws, Satan will cause you to feel worthless, discouraged, depressed, hopeless, unmotivated, unworthy, and useless; Heavenly Father will cause the feelings of "I can do this; I need to take another step forward; give me another mountain to climb." Heavenly Father will build you up. The feelings of humble confidence, optimism, excitement, and exhilaration for the challenge are all indications that the Lord is coaxing you to improve yourself and to take the next important step on your pathway to exaltation.

Not only will this be a valuable lesson to learn, but you can also bless the lives of your companions, members, and investigators. Too many people act like lost puppies, believing they have sinned, when they should actually be jubilant because our Heavenly Father wants them to take on their next great challenge. Your ability to discern the difference in why the Spirit leaves could save you and many others a lot of worry and wasted time. Knowing the difference will also help you to make other major decisions correctly for the rest of your life.

The Blessings of 100 Percent Obedience

I, THE LORD, AM BOUND WHEN ye do what I say; but when ye do not what I say, ye have no promise" (D&C 82:10). What a breath of fresh air to meet a new missionary who does not have his or her own rule book. When you signed your acceptance letter, you told the prophet in effect, "I will go where you want me to go," and "I will do what you want me to do." Don't go back on your commitment!

Every missionary who got off the plane seemed to be 100 percent committed to keeping the commandments and the mission rules. During their first day in the mission, they committed to continue to be "MTC obedient." The excitement level was high, and we felt that these were the ones who would conquer the world. During their first round of zone conferences, I interviewed each of them. They would express their commitment to total obedience. I would commend and encourage them.

By the second month, they had discovered how difficult it is to obey *all* the rules, especially if their trainers or fellow missionaries were more relaxed than they had committed to be. Many were still determined to set a record for obedience. By the third month, they had experienced their share of hard times: difficult areas, challenging companions, frustrating news from home, rejection by investigators, and the pressure of learning all they were required to learn.

At this point the men were separated from the boys, and the women from the girls. The true missionaries of Christ were determined enough and strong enough to reach their goal of 100 percent obedience in spite of the difficulty of the task. The others started making excuses why they couldn't keep all the mission rules. "Nobody else is totally obedient" was one of the most frequently used rebuttals. "My companion and others tease me because I'm trying to obey all the rules, which bothers me. And I just don't understand why this stupid rule is here. I'm not going to live dumb rules"—these are two other weak attempts to justify disobedience. I would remind these missionaries that the Lord never said, "I the Lord am bound if ye do 80 percent of what I say"! If faithful missionaries want the Lord to bless them as promised, they need to be 100 percent obedient.

When these missionaries attempted to rationalize that "nobody keeps all the rules," I would ask them to identify any rule they felt was impossible to keep. I would then promise them that I would excuse them from following those rules. Never once in three years did a missionary suggest a rule that could not be kept. Obedience is a matter of deciding you will just *do it*—no excuses, no arguments, no rationalization, just plain obedience.

Many years ago, the Sunday School class I was in had gained a reputation for being rowdy. One particular Sunday we were really on a roll. We had gone through three teachers before the class was half over. The fourth teacher was a kind, Christlike grandma we all knew well. I guess our destructive momentum was just too great—she left in tears within a few minutes. We were all pleased with our accomplishment until the bishop walked in. There was dead silence. He scanned our semicircle of chairs, starting on the opposite end from me. He stopped in front of every child and stared into his or her eyes. When he got to me, he stared into my eyes and asked, "Randy, why do you act like that?" I used the typical excuse, "Why are you picking on me? Everybody else was doing it too!" He then shocked us all by responding, "Shut up! You know better than that. Don't ever use that excuse as long as you live!" I knew I was in trouble. I knew that he was telling the truth. Misbehavior on the part of everyone else in the world was no excuse for me. I am grateful for the courage of that bishop.

Mission president Alma taught the same truth in chastising his wayward missionary son, Corianton: "Yea, she did steal away the hearts of many; but this was no excuse for thee, my son" (Alma 39:4). Joseph Smith was bluntly taught the same lesson by the Lord, who said: "Behold, you should not have feared man more than God. Although men set at naught the counsels of God, and despise his words—yet you should have been faithful; and he would have extended his arm and supported you against all the fiery darts of the adversary; and he would have been with you in every time of trouble" (D&C 3:7–8). If you want to maintain static-free communication between you and the Lord, you must not compromise your commitment to total obedience.

What if you don't understand the "whys" behind a mission rule? Live it until you can get an answer from the mission president. Remember the response of our faithful father Adam when the angel asked him why he offered sacrifices: "I know not, save the Lord commanded me" (Moses 5:6). An explanation followed that put everything in proper perspective. But remember that Adam obeyed until he understood because he had explicit faith in the Lord.

What do you do if your companion or fellow missionaries are breaking the rules? Try to reason with them. Explain how they are not only hurting themselves but also slowing down the work. Although they have made the same commitments you have, their reactions may surprise you. They may mock you, tease you, try to persuade you to join them, or ignore you. But rest assured that they know, deep down inside, that you are right and that they should be obedient. It is rather ironic that others will mock you for doing the very thing to which they committed themselves. Being obedient is never easy or even popular. But "strait is the gate, and narrow is the way, which leadeth unto life, and few there be that find it" (Matthew 7:14).

It is funny how quickly we excuse our shortcomings when nobody else is living the way they should. In the long run, those who are led back to the right path will thank you for setting a good example. In the Old Testament, Ezekiel suggests that you actually have a responsibility to warn others:

> Again, when a righteous man doth turn from his righteousness, and commit iniquity, and I lay a stumbling block before him, he shall die: because thou hast not given him warning, he shall die in his sin, and his righteousness which he hath done shall not be remembered; but his blood will I require at thine hand.
>
> Nevertheless if thou warn the righteous man, that the righteous sin not, and he doth not sin, he shall surely live, because he is warned; also thou hast delivered thy soul (Ezekiel 3:20–21).

22

STAYING WORTHY

IT WOULD SEEM OBVIOUS THAT a missionary is worthy to serve, but you may not be prepared for the adversary's clever attempts to destroy you. Satan and his evil forces will constantly attack you because you are a missionary. As you begin to fulfill your call to "hold up your light that it may shine unto the world" (3 Nephi 18:24) and share the gospel of Jesus Christ with others, you will find that your weaknesses become more apparent. Unresolved issues from your past may come back to haunt you, while other things that you hadn't even considered wrong may start to weigh on your mind.

The adversary wants you to believe that because you are not yet perfect, you really shouldn't serve a mission. This is just another of his lies, because Satan is "the spirit of that wicked one who was a liar from the beginning" (D&C 93:25). The Lord uses the sanctifying process of personal revelation—line upon line and precept upon precept. Remember that the Spirit leaves for two reasons: because the Lord is coaxing you to move ahead, or because you are sinning.

If the Lord were to show us, all at once, everything we need to do to qualify for the celestial kingdom, we would probably become discouraged and quit. But a mission represents a unique opportunity. Never before in your life have you focused with such intensity on personal worthiness. As you do this, it becomes painfully evident that you are not the kind of a person you should be. In other words, as you hold up the light to lead others to Christ, it illuminates every flaw in your armor.

Prepare yourself for this to happen. How will you handle those feelings of hypocrisy? It is very simple. You should not regard yourself as someone who has "arrived." You still struggle, as does the rest of humanity. When you invite others to follow your example, you are merely saying, "Follow me as I am trying to follow the Savior. When I stumble, help me to get up; don't criticize me for being imperfect. I'm doing the best I can. You help me and I'll help you, and together we'll both become better people."

There is a fine line between being too hard on yourself and being too lenient. Only the presence of the Spirit can tell you when you are on the right course. If you begin to tell yourself you can never do anything right, you need to reevaluate. If you never select areas for improvement, you also need to reconsider. No missionary is totally bad or totally good. We are all on the journey of life toward perfection.

When you do slip and break a rule, don't stay down. Repent immediately and ask your Heavenly Father for forgiveness. He will let you know that your repentance has been accepted when the Spirit returns. He is willing then to shift the responsibility for payment for your sins onto the Savior. If you happen to break a bigger rule or commandment, one that might jeopardize your worthiness to serve, immediately contact the mission president. To leave the problem unresolved will only result in greater condemnation because you will be serving unworthily.

When you contact the mission president, be honest and

to the point. Tell him exactly what happened. To speak in generalities doesn't help anyone. In order to make a correct judgment, the mission president needs to know all the facts. Unless the transgression is really very serious, you will not be sent home. If you are, it will be for your eternal welfare.

How do you know when to involve the mission president? Basically, if you cannot (being totally honest with yourself) get the Spirit back after you have confessed to the Lord, you probably need to talk to the president. Remember, your Heavenly Father is very eager to have you serve an honorable mission. Therefore, he considers a missionary's past, present, and future as one eternal "now." Your eternal well-being is more important to him than your temporary embarrassment. Whatever the Spirit prompts you to do, do it. The reason you are talking to the mission president is because the keys of judgment have been given to him. He can make an objective judgment, as well as feel genuine concern for your plight. He will seem more like a loving father than a harsh judge. Whatever his decision, it will be the best for you.

The adversary wants you to be preoccupied with being sent home. He may even urge you to tell the president about your past, even though you cleared it up with your home bishop and stake president. Usually there is no need to uncover these pardoned transgressions. If you think the bishop or stake president perhaps made a mistake or didn't get all the information he needed, let the mistake lie with the bishop or stake president.

Frequently, the adversary confuses a righteous missionary by planting doubts about his or her repentance process. Then he suggests that maybe you'd better confess again. So after you talk to the mission president, everything is fine for a couple of days. But you think of one more twist that you forgot to tell him. Satan will suggest that you'd better make a special appointment and get rid of everything. Another special interview with the mission president helps you relax for awhile. However, the cycle repeats itself until you realize, or the mission president identifies, what the adversary is doing. The disease is called "confessionitis." It is not common, but if you have it, you need to conquer the problem. During an interview, explain to the president that you want to be totally clean from the past. You are willing to empty the bucket of former sins once and for all. After you have finished the confession, ask the Lord if there is anything else that needs to be discussed. Explain that you are more than willing to do whatever he requires, but it should be revealed now rather than every other week. Ask the Lord, in his infinite wisdom, what he would have you do. When the feelings of "what to do next" are gone, you may assume you have completed the process and should move on with your life.

The next time the adversary tries to dredge up the past, command him to leave. Explain that you don't have five minutes to waste on his lies. You have exaltation to gain. Move forward positively and optimistically. Those feelings of despair will leave, and you will progress toward your eternal goal. Will you still remember past transgressions? Yes. Will you still regret having committed them? Yes, definitely. Will you still have that gut-wrenching fear of being in the presence of the Lord? No, that will be gone forever. In the words of one who knows and is willing to describe it for us, Alma says, "Behold, when I thought this [about the Savior and his atonement], I could remember my pains no more; yea, I was harrowed up by the memory of my sins no more. And oh, what joy, and what marvelous light I did behold; yea, my soul was filled with joy as exceeding as was my pain!"

(Alma 36:19–20.) Alma does not say he did not remember having sinned, but he did say that the pain was gone, and he was not continually "harrowed up" by the memory of his past transgressions. We can and should enjoy the same blessings concerning our past transgressions.

Enos, who prayed all day long and into the night before he received a remission of his past sins, described it this way: "I, Enos, knew that God could not lie; wherefore, my guilt was swept away" (Enos 1:6). The people who listened to aged King Benjamin had one of those "forgiving experiences." It is recorded like this: "And it came to pass that after they had spoken these words [asking for the atoning blood of Christ to cleanse them] the Spirit of the Lord came upon them, and they were filled with joy, having received a remission of their sins, and having peace of conscience" (Mosiah 4:3). Neither Enos nor the people of King Benjamin claimed to have forgotten their past sins, but both described a relief from guilt and a peace of conscience that accompanied the remission of their sins.

Perhaps we have been fooled again by Satan to expect a false set of conditions to indicate a remission of our sins. You are worthy to serve when you have the Spirit. You are worthy to serve when your mission president, knowing all he needs to know about your past, says you are worthy to serve.

There is a certain irony in the way Satan works. He tells you that you are totally worthless, yet he doubles his efforts against your influence, talent, and potential. This approach doesn't seem appropriate if he really considers you a loser. Either you pose a real threat to him and his kingdom or you do not. Satan can't have it both ways.

I have found that the "zoom out" tactic is very beneficial. Step back from your situation and consider the big picture.

Of all the commandments the Lord has given, how many do you live? Probably 95 to 99 percent. In fact, probably only a couple of commandments cause you to struggle. If you got 99 percent or even 95 percent on a test, would you consider yourself a total failure? Of course not. No, you are not trying to excuse less-than-perfect performance, but neither are you ready to give up because you missed one small part of the test. Before you retried the test, you would probably look to see which questions you missed so you could correct them. Your attitude toward weaknesses should be the same.

Years ago, I was thinning sugar beets for a farmer. The rows were long and the hoe handle was short. It required that I bend over for hours at a time. I remember looking at the end of the row and thinking I would never make it. I must have looked discouraged, because the farmer brought me a bottle of warm water. He was not a man of many words, but he did say, "Look how far you've come!" When I looked back, I was surprised. I had come a long way. Several times during the following hours, I looked back to see how far I had come. Occasionally, we need to give ourselves credit for how far we've come so that we gain added strength to continue the battle.

If you serve honorably, you will foil the evil programs used by the adversary. Because of your faithfulness, he will do all he can to convince you that you cannot serve because you are not yet perfect. Listen to the Good Shepherd and his chosen leaders, not to the "liar from the beginning" (D&C 93:25).

23

TEACH, TEACH, TEACH

AS A MISSIONARY, YOU ARE sent forth for one purpose—to teach. How and what to teach will be a challenge for your entire mission. Let's start by broadening your vision of *whom* you are to teach. You might say you are to teach nonmembers the six standard discussions. True, but it hardly describes the scope of your stewardship. Let's consider some other areas of responsibility.

First, you are under divine command to *teach yourself.* Almost a year before the Church was formally organized in this dispensation, Hyrum Smith felt a great urge to share the gospel with others. The Lord gave Hyrum's younger brother, Joseph, a revelation for Hyrum, which reads:

> Seek not to declare my word, but first seek to obtain my word, and then shall your tongue be loosed; then, if you desire, you shall have my Spirit and my word, yea, the power of God unto the convincing of men.
>
> But now hold your peace; study my word which hath gone forth among the children of men, and also study my word which shall come forth among the children of men, . . . until you have obtained all which I shall grant unto the children of men in this generation, and then shall all things be added thereto (D&C 11:21–22).

In teaching yourself, you will discover quickly the holes in your understanding of the gospel. If you were so unwise as to waste your youth (and so many of us did!), then you will have to redouble your efforts to catch up. On the day I arrived in Samoa for my first mission, the elders who met the plane took me to visit an old Catholic priest. I did not know they did this with all new missionaries. After the introductions were over, this good man kindly (sometimes not so kindly) beat me about the head and shoulders with my own doctrine. He knew much more about what I believed and where it was found in the scriptures than I did. I felt like a total failure. Had there been a plane heading back to the United States, I probably would have been on it. But since there was only a weekly flight to Hawaii, I was stuck. So I determined at that time never again to be embarrassed like that. I started an intensive study program that has continued for the twenty-nine years since then and will likely continue until death halts my earthly study. When you are not preaching, spend your time studying the gospel. Study the scriptures ("my word which hath gone forth") and the teachings of the latter-day prophets ("my word which shall come forth"). Once you master the scriptures and the teachings of the latter-day prophets, you can broaden your study to other sources—but this will likely not happen while you are in the mission.

Next, you have a responsibility to teach your companion. As a "greeny," you may think your trainer has the sole responsibility to teach you. In many things that will be true. He or she has served longer, has more experience, and is therefore more qualified to teach you the practical points of effective missionary work. But no trainers have perfected themselves to the point that they have no need to continue learning. Perhaps they come from a less-active family and have little background in the gospel or how to live success-fully in a family. If you have expertise in areas where your trainer is lacking, don't be shy about sharing your under-standing with him or her.

After you've been in the mission awhile, you'll discover that there are no perfect missionaries. Every time you get a chance to share the truths you take as commonplace, the Spirit will lift you up. Be careful not to come across as a know-it-all. No one likes to be talked down to or treated like a little kid. In Doctrine and Covenants 43:8 the Lord com-mands, "I give unto you a commandment, that when ye are assembled together ye shall instruct and edify each other, that ye may know how to act and direct my church, how to act upon the points of my law and commandments, which I have given." The discussions provide golden opportunities to share your insight without the tone of preachiness. Sometimes, waiting until your advice is sought is infinitely more effective than trying to interject your thoughts when they are not welcomed. Be sensitive to the promptings of the Spirit.

Believe it or not, you are also responsible to teach the members. Many of them are eager to do member-missionary work, but they just don't know how. It is a natural reaction to become frustrated at their lack of know-how. But remember that a natural reaction is not necessarily correct. "The natural man is an enemy to God" (Mosiah 3:19). Come down off your high horse and assume that people are basically good and want to do what their Heavenly Father expects of them. Whenever members foul up, it is to your advantage to give them the benefit of a doubt. Step back, as philosophers do, and ask, "Is there a prior question?" In plain English that means, "Is there something even more basic that I need to explain so they can successfully do what I am asking them to do?" If you train your mind to ask "prior questions," you will almost always find some point you need to teach or reteach. Be very careful not to come across as the hypocritically pious, more-holy-than-thou missionary who passes out tidbits of celestial counsel. Be humble and sincere in your approach. People respond warmly when they perceive that you are genuinely interested and are trying to help. They will shut you off in a minute if they feel you are condescending or insincere in your attempts to help. You should never tire of trying to help others do better. Remember, your Heavenly Father (whom you represent) did not give up on you, even though as you look back on your youth, you may not understand why he didn't!

Included in the member group you are to teach are priesthood leaders and other officers. The bishop, a very busy man, wants to be totally successful. The fact that he doesn't devote every meeting to missionary work does not mean he is not interested. He may not know how to integrate missionary work into his regular schedule. Here is where you can offer to help. Don't demand time in the priesthood executive committee (PEC) meeting or the ward correlation council (WCC). Suggest to the bishop that you have some ideas you would like to share with the leaders of the ward at a convenient time. You might be surprised how receptive the bishop is to your teaching.

As you work with the ward mission leader, you may be tempted to criticize him because "he's a returned missionary and should know better!" He may have been back ten years and is struggling to keep his family fed, clothed, and housed. The pressures of his postmission experience may have left very little time to be involved in missionary-related activities. He may even doubt his effectiveness as a missionary. Build him up; make him look good; give him ideas on how to involve the entire ward. Do not become his adversary. If he becomes your enemy, you can cancel your plans for nightly dinner appointments, forget getting members to go on companion exchanges, commonly called splits, with you and your companion, and dismiss the idea of member referrals. Without the assistance of the ward mission leader, you will be at best only marginally successful. Even if you baptized a dozen people without the ward mission leader's help, who knows how many other people you might have been able to reach *with* his help. You may use the same rationale with the Relief Society president, the Young Men president, and the elders quorum president—all key people who can make or break your efforts in the ward. Even though missionaries were there years before you arrived, you may still have a massive teaching job before the ward functions the way the Lord intended.

Nonmembers or prospective members constitute what you may have viewed as your primary teaching role. There are generally thousands of them in your area. The problem is finding those who are prepared to be taught. How can you recognize them? The Lord gives the answer in Doctrine and Covenants 35:12: "There are none that doeth good except those who are ready to receive the fulness of my gospel, which I have sent forth unto this generation." Look for those who go quietly about doing good. The news media floods us with stories of murder, gang violence, and scams. Contrary to common belief, criminals do not constitute a majority of the population. I prefer to believe the Lord's promise, "There are many yet on the earth among all sects, parties, and denominations, who are blinded by the subtle craftiness of men, whereby they lie in wait to deceive, and who are only kept from the truth because they know not where to find it" (D&C 123:12).

If you can learn to look at your fellow sojourners on earth the way the Lord does, your approach to them will be entirely different. A familiar scripture suggests that we "remember the worth of souls is great in the sight of God" (D&C 18:10). How great is that worth? This question helps me to think in terms of potential. How much money would it take to "buy" God? You may think this is a ridiculous question. But remember, every person on earth has the potential to become like our Heavenly Father. For you to say, "Oh, that person is a waste of our time" is to say that the Savior's atonement was in vain. Remember again, "The Lord your Redeemer suffered death in the flesh; wherefore he suffered the pain of all men, that all men might repent and come unto him" (D&C 18:11).

Some investigators are presently more prepared to receive the gospel than others. Learn to use your time most productively. When you are not formally teaching a discussion, teach, teach, teach whomever will listen. The great condemnation given by the Lord to the missionaries is this: "With some I am not well pleased, for they will not open their mouths, but they hide the talent which I have given them, because of the fear of man. Wo unto such, for mine anger is kindled against them. And it shall come to pass, if they are not more faithful unto me, it shall be taken away, even that which they have" (D&C 60:2–3). I don't know of any missionaries who died from teaching too many people. However, some thought they would die of boredom because they did not share their knowledge of the gospel with others.

Alma, in trying to prepare his sons for missionary work, taught Shiblon, "Use boldness, but not overbearance" (Alma 38:12). In our zeal to make rapid progress, we sometimes fail to respect others' agency. Not every nonmember will accept the gospel. Not every member or leader will implement your teachings and become more effective in member-missionary work. Not all of your companions and fellow missionaries will heed your counsel and become more Christlike. Many will not—but some will.

What should you teach? The Lord is firm and clear in his directions: "And again, the elders, priests and teachers of this church shall teach the principles of my gospel, which are in the Bible and the Book of Mormon, in the which is the fulness of the gospel" (D&C 42:12). Why doesn't he mention the Doctrine and Covenants and the Pearl of Great Price? The answer is that they weren't yet published when the revelation was given. His unmistakable counsel is to teach "my gospel" from the scriptures. You are not sent forth to teach your personal ideas. You must teach the doctrine from the scriptures or from Latter-day prophets or not teach at all. The Lord put that restriction in place when he said, "Let them journey from thence preaching the word by the way, saying none other things than that which the prophets and apostles have written, and that which is taught them by the Comforter through the prayer of faith" (D&C 52:9). The Lord counseled the early brethren who wanted to teach their own ideas, "They shall give heed to that which is written, and pretend to no other revelation" (D&C 32:4).

The Lord, through the proper channels, has provided you with an official set of standard missionary discussions. Use these until they are modified by the Brethren. Many young missionaries have discovered to their embarrassment that the Brethren were wise in teaching only basic doctrines. One big mistake that missionaries make is trying to teach beyond the basics. Remember, you don't understand everything, and the investigator is just beginning to comprehend what is being taught.

Stick with the scriptures and the Brethren. If you fail to heed the counsel, you may learn by sad experience that the Lord knows what is best. For more than one hundred and sixty years, missionaries have been teaching the same basic gospel doctrine—and have had much success doing so.

In order to be more prepared, take the challenge to research, organize, and write two talks per month on a gospel topic. Prepare them as though you were going to be asked to present them in a zone conference, sacrament meeting, or stake conference. If you write them from the time you arrive, you would have forty-eight (or thirty-six for sisters) scripturally oriented talks at your fingertips. You will be prepared when asked at the last minute to speak, saving yourself apologies and embarrassment. Someday that "minuteman" preparedness will pay big dividends. In addition, your understanding of the dozens of topics will be much deeper and better researched than if you were to deliver an impromptu talk. Perhaps as a concluding remark, the Lord's charge is most appropriate: Teach the gospel from the scriptures by the power of the Spirit (see D&C 50:13–14). Follow this counsel, and you will be on solid ground when the floods of false doctrine rage around you.

24

....

WORKING WITH MEMBERS

ONE OF THE TRUE JOYS OF missionary work is learning to work with members. The significance of the work goes far beyond just being enjoyable. President Ezra Taft Benson said, "We need to understand that member-missionary work is literally the key to the future growth of the Church and that we have covenanted with our Father in Heaven to do this work" (Ezra Taft Benson, "President Kimball's Vision of Missionary Work," *Ensign*, July 1985, p. 11).

"We must emphasize the need for more member-missionary work. Experience has proven this is the most fruitful missionary work. Member-missionary work is one of the great keys to the individual growth of our members. It is my conviction that member-missionary work will raise the spirituality in any ward where applied" ("Strengthen the Stakes of Zion," El Paso Regional Conference, 25 January 1986; quoted in *The Teachings of Ezra Taft Benson*, Salt Lake City: Bookcraft, pp. 208–9).

These words are from a modern-day prophet. The most effective missionary work is that which includes members. However, working with members can be challenging and frustrating. No active members of the Church get up each morning and say to themselves, "I wonder what I can do to avoid doing missionary work today." If you assume that each member wants to be good and faithful, you are much more likely to have success.

Whenever investigators don't understand something, you are to teach them the correct doctrine until they understand. Why should it be any different with members? If members don't know how to do missionary work, teach them. You may assume that they already know how and just don't want to be involved, but that is usually not the case. Yes, they may be returned missionaries or bishops or hold some other responsible Church position. That does not automatically guarantee that they know how to share the gospel with their neighbors. Remember, the same opposition you feel from the adversary that tempts you not to be valiant in your missionary work is also working on the members.

How do you work with members? Start by earning their trust. It would be wonderful if the image of missionaries among the members was positive. In many areas that may be true. However, some missionaries have unfortunately given the rest a bad reputation. As a result, you will repeatedly have to prove by your actions that you are sincere and hardworking. Never step out of character—be diligent, friendly, warm, approachable, directed, sober, humble, and committed. As you radiate these qualities, members will see they can trust their close friends and family with you. On the other hand, if you are hotheaded, cold, unstable in Church doctrine, unlearned in the scriptures, lazy, or insincere, that too shows, and no one can in good conscience entrust their family and friends to your care. You must earn support from members.

You will rapidly discover that some members are justifiably tired of new member-missionary programs. Unless new programs are promoted through the mission, try to use existing programs to increase member participation in missionary work. New, short-lived programs are frustrating to members. Be careful that the methods you use to involve members do not require so much time that even the faithful see no way to complete your training sessions.

Teach the "hows" as well as the "whats" of missionary work. We are pretty good at telling people *what* to do. Don't do that unless you immediately follow up with an explanation of *how* to accomplish what you have asked. Because it seems obvious and simple to you, do not assume that everyone has the same vision. Be realistic! If what you ask members to do is so time-consuming that to be successful at it would require them to quit their jobs, you may well expect your approach to fail. For you, missionary work is a full-time commitment. They still have to worry about work, church, family, and their social lives.

Make member-missionary work fun. Avoid making members feel guilty for not being more diligent. Whenever you use guilt, threats, or negative reinforcement to achieve member involvement, everybody loses. Missionary work has built-in, positive rewards.

Set realistic time goals. It takes time to teach members how to overcome fears. Missionaries often want everything to happen immediately, but it doesn't work that way. It may take a month or longer to help a family get over their fear of asking their neighbors over for a family home evening. If you are not too concerned about who gets the "credit" for bringing people into the Church, you can do a lot of good. The true fruits of your service may be realized by missionaries who come after you. What an eternal reward you will receive for building a solid base of member-missionary activities. One of the true signs of spiritual maturity is to continue working diligently even when it is apparent that you will not be in the area long enough to reap the benefits of your hard work.

Don't try to move people faster than they are willing and able to move. The gauge is not when the missionaries are ready, but when the members are ready. You will discover that trying to move too quickly will have negative and long-lasting effects. It is better to move more slowly and make sure everyone is comfortable.

Trying to work with too many people at one time is not very effective either. Select five or six families who show the most promise for member involvement. Get them actively working, and then they in turn can involve two or three more families by training them to do member–missionary work. The work, like a snowball rolling down a slope, will start small and slowly. As time passes it will increase in size and speed. Be patient.

Work closely with the ward mission leader. Remember that the bishop is in charge of all three parts of the Church's mission: perfecting the Saints, redeeming the dead, and proclaiming the gospel. The ward mission leader is the bishop's right-hand man in ensuring that proclaiming the gospel receives proper attention. Not every ward mission leader has an expansive vision of his calling, just as not every missionary knows why he or she is serving a mission. If there is a lack of vision on the part of the bishop and ward mission leader, teach them. It is easy to criticize everything that isn't done exactly to your liking. A more spiritually mature approach is to help everyone approach the ideal by teaching and showing them the way.

The weekly correlation meeting with the ward mission leader can be a valuable time to make sure you are all on the same team. If you don't get along with the ward mission leader, you will probably not be very successful in the ward. If the weekly correlation meetings are not being held, gently suggest that you really need them. Ask for the ward mission leader's help. Make him feel important—he is! If you let him suggest a convenient time to meet, he will more likely attend the meetings. If he is reluctant to hold formal meetings, a five-minute meeting after sacrament meeting in the hallway is better than no meeting.

Let the ward mission leader know whom you are working with, and suggest that he ask for help from auxiliaries in friendshipping your investigators. In other words, provide him with some agenda items for PEC and WCC meetings. The ward mission leader is your liaison with your investigators and the ward organization and its resources. You can't possibly host enough socials, homemaking meetings, Primary programs, and Young Men and Young Women outings to meet the needs of your investigators. Without the help of the ward, your effectiveness is diminished.

Let the ward mission leader coordinate the ward's resources. Let him know how vital he is to the success of the missionary effort in the ward. A close working relationship with him makes your work more enjoyable and productive, while an adversarial relationship renders you ineffective and may cause you to be discouraged with the work. In the unlikely event that the ward mission leader will not cooperate at all, ask for an interview with the bishop. Explain what you have tried to do to work with the ward mission leader. Ask the bishop for suggestions. If that doesn't work, have your zone leader talk to the stake mission president, who can work through the proper priesthood channels and remedy the problem. Generally, the problem does not lie with the ward mission leader, but with missionaries who have treated him poorly in the past. He could be a little hesitant, and you may have to win his confidence just as you need to do with the members. He too wants to magnify his calling. It requires patience and perseverance to teach him how to do that.

Nothing will draw you closer to the members and the Lord than working together to "bring to pass the immortality and eternal life" of our Father's other children (Moses 1:39). Because of the potential for good when we are united, expect some opposition from the adversary and learn how to overcome it. The rewards will outweigh the challenges as you work with members.

ANSWERING QUESTIONS
WITHOUT BASHING

MOST OF THE PEOPLE YOU TEACH will be honestly seeking the truth. Their questions will be sincere, and they will accept your explanations. However, a few, some of whom may have taken debate in high school, are prepared to argue every comma and period. The tendency is to engage them to "prove the gospel." That never has worked and likely never will. Must you silently accept criticism? Not at all. You have the truth, and the truth will never change in spite of the arguments of the less informed. The following methods of responding may help you satisfy their immediate query so you can continue to teach the great saving truths of the Restoration.

1. Try to understand the person's question and where he or she is coming from. It may require that you ask some clarifying questions. Often we have an answer already prepared before we understand the question. A little silence won't hurt anyone. Sometimes it is helpful to rephrase the question to see if you understand, but be cautious about restating—unless you are sincere, it may sound as if you're mocking. Once you understand the question, you are ready to continue.

2. See if you can find a similar situation in the Bible. Perhaps an example will clarify this point. One of the questions frequently used to trap missionaries is that Mormon records that after Christ's crucifixion there was darkness in the Americas for three days and three nights (see 3 Nephi 8), while the New Testament clearly states that the darkness lasted only three hours (see Luke 23:44). Thus they see a glaring contradiction: Surely Joseph Smith made a fatal mistake when he wrote that the darkness lasted for three days in America. So goes the line of reasoning. Make sure you know their position by asking, "Are you saying the Book of Mormon can't be true because it records that the period of darkness lasted three days while Luke records it lasted only three hours?" Most will agree that is their concern. Ask them to consider the account of Moses and the ninth plague on Egypt—the plague of darkness. Exodus 10:21–29 clearly states that there was darkness for three days and three nights in all the land of Egypt, but that there was light in the land of Goshen (which is in the center of Egypt and where the children of Israel were) during the same period. I don't know how the Lord did it, but he did. Using contradictory evidence from the Bible shows that the person's argument may be faulty or illogical. The person may attempt to dismiss the contradictions of the Bible, but at the same time he is forced to admit that the same rationale could be used with so-called inconsistencies in modern-day scripture.

3. Avoid using apparent mistranslations in the Bible as the basis for your argument. You may be inclined to use the eighth article of faith—"We believe the Bible to be the word of God as far as it is translated correctly"—to justify inconsistencies. You may want to argue the construction of the Bible or the sequencing of the books in the Bible to support your point. But this is usually fruitless, since most people aren't familiar enough with Bible history to know whether what you say is correct. A prime example of this is Revelation 22:18–19. With almost the last stroke of his pen, the Apostle John forbids anyone to "take away from the words of the book of this prophecy" or to "add unto these things." Violators are warned that God will remove their names from the book of life or inflict upon them the plagues mentioned in the book of Revelation. It sounds pretty scary, and indeed it is. We can argue that other books of the New Testament were written after Revelation, which is true, and that "this book" refers only to Revelation and not to the entire Bible, which is also true. We may reason about the King James scholars and what was included as scripture and what wasn't. But these arguments aren't successful until a logical contradiction is created in the person's mind.

After making sure you understand the objection, you might say something like, "That sounds like anything added after that scripture is not approved of God. Is that what you mean?" The answer is usually yes, because the person honestly believes he or she is correct and is helping you to see the light. The cross-reference to Revelation 22:18 (see note 18a) suggests you turn to Deuteronomy 4:2, where you read something very similar to what is written in Revelation 22. After reading Deuteronomy 4:2, you might take all the pages between there and Revelation 22 in your hand and suggest that according to your critic's interpretation, what you are holding is not scripture and should be torn out and discarded. Of course the person will not agree. Most people either attempt no explanation at all, or they suggest an alternative meaning for Deuteronomy. This alternative suggestion is what you are looking for. Suggest that there is an explanation that makes Revelation and Deuteronomy non-contradictory. Then you can explain the sequential writing of the Bible and present those other arguments. You must lay the foundation before you try to put up the rafters and the roof.

It helps to recognize that intelligent people may struggle with that question. Acknowledge that the question is not a sign of inferior intelligence or lack of ability to reason. The answer simply requires more light and knowledge than the person presently has.

4. Use modern-day scriptures to teach the meaning of troublesome biblical passages. Mormon counseled us on how to use the Book of Mormon and other modern scripture to teach the skeptic. In Mormon 7:8–9 he says:

> Therefore repent, and be baptized in the name of Jesus, and lay hold upon the gospel of Christ, which shall be set before you, not only in this record but also in the record which shall come unto the Gentiles from the Jews, which record shall come from the Gentiles unto you.
>
> For behold, this [the Book of Mormon] is written for the intent that ye may believe that [the Bible]; and if ye believe that [the Bible] ye will believe this [the Book of Mormon] also; and if ye believe this [the Book of Mormon] ye will know concerning your fathers, and also the marvelous works which were wrought by the power of God among them.

Mormon provides the key to answering difficult questions. First find the answer in modern-day scripture. Then read the Bible and see what a difference it makes. For example, one of the most misunderstood but vital doctrines is the nature of God. Indeed, the Savior said it is "life eternal, that they might know thee the only true God, and Jesus Christ, whom thou hast sent" (John 17:3). The problem arises when we testify that God has a tangible body, because John 4:24 says that "God is a Spirit."

It takes some study, but your search is rewarded as you discover Doctrine and Covenants 130:22, which says in part: "The Father has a body of flesh and bones as tangible as man's." That is the true doctrine. Now to solve the apparent problem. John 4:24 states in full, "God is a Spirit: and they that worship him must worship him in spirit and in truth." Does the fact that God has a body prevent him from also having a spirit? Of course not. A thorough search reveals that "man is spirit. The elements are eternal, and spirit and element, inseparably connected, receive a fulness of joy" (D&C 93:33). Our spirits communicate with God's spirit: we do not have to rely solely on our physical eyes and ears. Man certainly does not have to lay aside his body so that his spirit can communicate with God. Likewise, God's ability to communicate with man's spirit does not require that he not have a body. Physically, God can only be in one place at one time, so it would be restrictive if he were limited to a physical means of communication. The Savior, in teaching the woman at the well in Samaria, said, "Ye worship ye know not what: we know what we worship" (John 4:22). If we wanted to continue our explanation from the Bible using our understanding gained from Doctrine and Covenants 130, we could use Luke 24:36–39 to show that the resurrected Christ had a body of flesh and bone that he invited the disciples to handle. Also, in Hebrews 1:1–3, Paul informs us that the Son is in the "express image" of the Father—meaning that he does not vary in any way. Together these scriptures clearly confirm what God has chosen to reveal about himself through modern-day prophets. You would miss a golden opportunity if you did not bear your testimony and express your thankfulness to the Lord for revealing such clear and unmistakable truths through modern prophets. The more you realize how blessed we are by doctrine that we tend to take for granted, the more powerful your witness will become.

In the early days of the Church, the Lord cautioned the missionaries not to try to debate with people by using our understanding of the Bible alone: "And my servant Leman shall be ordained unto this work, that he may reason with them, not according to that which he has received of them, but according to that which shall be taught him by you my servants; and by so doing I will bless him, otherwise he shall not prosper" (D&C 49:4). Debating doctrine using only the Bible will not cause us to prosper; using restoration scriptures will.

5. Keep attention focused on the true source of knowledge about the truthfulness of the Church. Often when bombarded by anti-Mormon literature or questions, the missionaries may feel that the burden of proof lies with them. While every missionary should learn how to answer questions put to him, the Church is not proven true or false based on that answer. Let me propose a useful dialogue when confronted with argumentative questions. After the question has been asked, you might say: "Suppose I can answer every one of your questions to your complete satisfaction. Does that automatically make the Church true?" The obvious answer is no. "Now suppose that I can't answer a single one of your questions, but that in the spirit of really wanting to know, you follow our challenge to 'ask of God' as James 1:5

directs and God answers your prayer in an unmistakable way. Does the fact that I cannot answer your questions make the Church incorrect when God testifies that it is true?" Again, the obvious answer is no. Then confirm that the Church is neither true nor false based on your ability to answer their questions. The truthfulness of the gospel depends on whether God reveals to the humble soul who asks, just like he promised in James 1:5 and Moroni 10:3–5.

6. Bear your testimony humbly and powerfully. Skeptics may debate the meaning of certain phrases, but no one can argue with your testimony. They may choose to disregard it or deny it, but it is personal and is not subject to debate. What you know and how you know it are very personal. You will do well to gain a testimony on every point of doctrine so you may speak as one having authority. Don't be afraid because you lack an advanced degree. Remember that God has called you, and he has promised that "no weapon that is formed against you shall prosper; and if any man lift his voice against you he shall be confounded in mine own due time" (D&C 71:9–10).

26

············

TRANSFERS

IT IS ONE OF THE SAD FACTS OF mission life that sooner or later you will be transferred from an area you have grown to love to a new area. The people in the old area have become like your own family. You know them well, and they know you well. You probably feel sure that the new area will never measure up to the one you just left. There will undoubtedly be people who have had a major impact on you and with whom you will want to keep in touch for the rest of your life.

First let's examine the positive factors in being transferred. If you are normal, you probably have a few faults that you are still trying to overcome. When you move to a new area, you start with a clean slate. No one knows how much experience you have had, or what you do well in, or where you fall short. Now is a good time for you to change. For example, in your first area you are known as "the greeny." Everyone knows you just arrived from the MTC, and consciously or not, they tend to treat you as if you don't know very much (probably because you don't!). As the months pass and you become more experienced, your confidence grows and you begin to mature as a missionary. However, certain members may always consider you to be the same as when you arrived. They are not confident in your ability to teach their family or friends. Although it isn't right, sometimes that's the way it is. There isn't any difference between the last day in your previous area and the first day in your current area. However, in the new area people consider you a full-fledged missionary with all the talents necessary to teach anyone they find. For that reason you'll be glad to move.

You may have developed some ties in the former area that were not necessarily unhealthy but that in time could develop into problems. Girls and guys tend to be attracted to the elders and to the sister missionaries. They actually love the spirit you radiate if you honor your calling. Because of a lack of understanding, these feelings may be misinterpreted as romantic love. Also, some of the older couples may have "adopted" you as their son or daughter. They may be so comfortable with you that they offer you the use of their home and everything in it. It is wise not to accept such offers. Too much familiarity lessens your effectiveness as a missionary. Frequent transfers keep these relationships on a more professional level.

Some individuals in the former area may have personality conflicts with you. Instead of approaching you personally and working things out, they may have taken the easy route and talked to others about you behind your back. A transfer gives you a fresh start. If you know what you were doing that caused them to dislike you, then you can avoid making the same mistakes in your next area.

If you were serving in a rather small geographic area, it may be that you have contacted everyone several times. Your personality will click with certain investigators and members and not with others. When you transfer to a new area, you can positively affect a new group of people. Let the mission president decide by inspiration when you have served long enough in an area. In your weekly letter to your president, tell him how you are doing and describe your relationships with companions and ward members, but don't tell him when you need a transfer. Before you leave that area, you may need to learn some valuable lessons that will help you for the rest of your life.

Usually you will love your current area and will not want to be transferred. When you get the transfer call, you will want to say farewell to your friends and investigators. Don't make your departure a theatrical affair. Sometimes people want to throw a farewell party for you. If you happen to be serving among people who have very limited resources (which includes most of the world!), they may spend all they have on a feast or present. Be cautious and sensitive about allowing them to do that. If you suspect they may react that way, wait until the morning of the transfer before informing them. Then graciously decline the invitation to let them spend all their money on you. Some people may be heartbroken to see you go. They may want you to stay, and some may even want to call the mission president to try to change his mind. Many times I received desperate calls from branch members pleading with me to leave an elder or sister in a particular area. They claimed the branch would fall apart if the missionary were transferred. I assured them that another equally fine missionary would be replacing their missionary and that everything would be all right. Several months later, when it was time to transfer the replacement missionary, I would again receive phone calls from members pleading that I would let the missionary stay. Let the Lord run the mission, and you will find that the Church moves forward, not backward.

Occasionally an elder or a sister would call and explain

that unusual circumstances required their continued service in an area. I learned early that no one is indispensable. The missionaries would be transferred as planned, and at the end of their mission, they would be amazed at how the branch or area had progressed in their absence.

People will almost always want to keep in touch with you. However, the white handbook clearly explains (for a very good reason) that you are not to write letters to, receive letters from, or have any unnecessary telephone communications with members residing within the boundaries of your mission. You must kindly and gently explain the rules. The problem will come when they inform you that other missionaries gave their new address and phone number. You might explain that your success on a mission is determined by how closely you follow the rules. If they really love you, they will not ask you to break the rules, because doing so deprives you of a portion of the Lord's Spirit. Most of them will readily understand and be more than willing to help you be obedient. It would be wonderful if every missionary would live the rules so that the members wouldn't be confused about whether they could or could not correspond with missionaries during their missions. Tell people you will contact them at the end of your mission. Give them your home address.

To know the wisdom of the rules, you will only have to serve in one area in which former missionaries violated the rules. Of course, members will be closer to someone who has served in their area six months than they will with you when you first arrive. If the members correspond with a former missionary who is willing to indulge them in their criticism that "the missionary who is here now doesn't love us like you did," you will find it nearly impossible to gain their confidence and trust as quickly as you otherwise could. As a mission president, I occasionally had to call local Church leaders and ask them to request that their members not call, write, or visit missionaries who had formerly served there, because those members were hindering the work.

Such members are not bad—it is only natural to want to stay close to those we love. But when they don't understand the rules, it is difficult to gain their support. Do yourself and those who follow you a favor: explain before you go what the rule is and why it is so important. Some missionaries are so insecure that they welcome affection from members in former areas. These missionaries don't quit until they see how detrimental their continued correspondence (phone calls, letters, or visits from members of the former area) is to the progress of the work. I would be afraid to stand before the Savior and try to explain why I accepted inappropriate affections at the expense of the progress of his work. Remember why you are serving a mission—it is to bring honor to him and not to yourself.

If a member writes to you from a former area, ask your mission president how to handle the problem. In our mission the missionary would explain the rules on a postcard and then send it to me at the mission office. I would forward it to the person along with a cover letter asking that person to help our missionaries be obedient. For the overwhelming majority of the time, this was effective. If it didn't work, I would request that the missionary mark "Refused, return to sender" on the letter and put it back into the mailbox. That always worked. That may seem a bit harsh, but your allegiance needs to be to your Heavenly Father and not to individual members.

If you are so irresistible that those of the opposite sex

can't leave you alone, you have a special problem. If you receive an unexpected and unwanted visit from someone in your area, call the mission president immediately and let him know what has happened. If there are romantic feelings between you and the other person, let the mission president know. It is far better for you to finish an honorable mission somewhere else than to return home without honor, and possibly without your membership, to the disgrace of yourself and your family. These instances are rare, but they do happen. The adversary will take advantage of every natural emotion to disrupt your mission and destroy you. Keep your guard up.

Finally, don't pine away for the area you just left. Close that chapter of your mission. Glory in the Lord that you have been privileged to meet so many neat people and enjoy such wonderful experiences. But go on with your life. In addition, when you get to your new area, don't compare it to your former area. No one likes to hear, "Well, this is the way we did it in my last area!" or "You people are not as faithful as the people in my last area!" If you want to destroy a potential relationship with the people in your new area, compare them to members in your former area. Enjoy each area for its own sake. Sure, second grade math was different from first grade math. One wasn't necessarily better than the other—just different. There will be new lessons to learn in this area, just as there were lessons to learn in your former area. They may be different lessons altogether. That doesn't make one area bad and the other good. They are just different.

You will find this to be good counsel when you return home and start to compare your mission with the missions of your friends. They will be as different as can be. Not better or worse—just different.

Not Speaking Ill of Others

It is difficult to believe that some missionaries are really missionaries. Their attitude needs a major overhaul, their manner of dress and conduct is not appropriate and their lack of focus on the work is apparent. The shock comes when you learn that some other missionaries are saying the same things about you!

The scriptures plainly teach that we see in others our own weaknesses. Paul taught in Romans 2:1: "Thou art inexcusable, O man, whosoever thou art that judgest: for wherein thou judgest another, thou condemnest thyself; for thou that judgest doest the same things." Many people have the habit of judging others. It is easy to stand back and pass judgment on everyone and everything. Too often we use ourselves as the standard against which everything else is judged. If you view everyone who is different from you as strange, you will see that the entire world is strange because you are unique.

Unless you are assigned to work in an area where missionaries have never labored before, you are bound to hear stories about the missionaries who were there before. Be very careful not to fall into the gossip trap. Even if everything you are told is true, it doesn't do any good to spread gossip. You don't have to live very long before you discover that you can't please all the people all of the time. Someone will always see things differently than you do. Some will differ from you politically. Some will interpret scriptures differently than you do. Some will have different tastes in clothing and hairstyles. The list is endless.

Whenever you speak unkindly about other missionaries, you damage the very cause you were sent to promote. That does not mean you have to lie about missionaries who have acted inappropriately. You are not obligated to say anything at all. Consider asking the following questions before you pass on any information. First ask yourself, "Is it true?" If you don't know for sure that something is true, it would be better left unsaid. Secondhand information is often either distorted or completely wrong. Second, "Is it kind?" Certain information may be true, but the effects of passing it on could be devastating. For example, say that an elder has made a serious moral mistake and has to return home as part of the repentance process. You are transferred into the area. The mission president has shared just enough of the problem to keep you from making the same mistake. Someone asks you if you know what happened to the elder. In truth you know what happened. However, it is better to say nothing at all, both for his sake and for the sake of missionary work itself. Third, "Is it necessary?" Even if something is true and kind, it may not be necessary for you to pass it on. People spend too much time gossiping while the necessary work of the kingdom is put on the back burner. You and your companion are often in the best position to know what is going on in the lives of members and nonmembers alike. If you make the mistake of being the communication center for the ward, you will find that all your time is spent talking about other people. When the Lord commanded, "Say nothing but repentance unto this generation" (D&C 11:9), he sent an unmistakable message that our time should be focused entirely on him and his gospel.

Another thing that helped me and my missionaries focus on things that are important is the saying "Small minds talk about people; average minds talk about things; great minds talk about ideas." What would happen if we refused to allow our minds to be either small or average but insisted on having great minds? Many great ideas, eternal principles, and soul-expanding concepts go unattended because we are too focused on gossip.

You may have come from a small farming community where everybody knew everything about everybody. You will find it difficult to break a lifelong habit. But it is possible, and the rewards are worth the effort. Catch yourself or have your companion call you up short if you start to talk about others. If you are serving in an area where gossip is prevalent, it is doubly difficult to break the cycle. Be open, honest, and frank about wanting to avoid the practice. In stating your desire to quit gossiping, don't label or belittle the local people. Ask for their assistance. By their helping you, they may come to realize that they too need to make some adjustments. Just one righteous man or woman can make a big difference.

The Book of Mormon tells the story of the powerful, transforming influence of one righteous man among people who had gone astray.

> Now this Melchizedek was a king over the land of Salem; and his people had waxed strong in iniquity and abomination; yea, they had all gone astray; they were full of all manner of wickedness.
>
> But Melchizedek having exercised mighty faith, and received the office of the high priesthood according to

the holy order of God, did preach repentance unto his people. And behold, they did repent; and Melchizedek did establish peace in the land in his days; therefore he was called the prince of peace, for he was the king of Salem; and he did reign under his father. (Alma 13:17–18)

With a little substitution, this scripture gives us a clear program for helping the local people perfect themselves. Substitute your name for Melchizedek. The modified version may read: "Now [your name] was an elder/sister over the land of [city where you serve]; and the members had waxed strong in iniquity and gossip; yea, they had all gone astray; they were full of all manner of wickedness. But [your name] having exercised mighty faith, and received the office of missionary according to the calling from the Prophet, did preach the peaceable way to live unto the people in the ward. And behold, they did repent [change!]; and [your name] did establish peace in the ward in his/her stay there as a missionary; therefore [your name] was called blessed by the people, for he/she did serve with honor under the direction of the mission president."

It may be that you can't change the entire mission—but maybe you can. You will never know the impact you have had until you have served your entire mission the way you know you should. It will probably require a rerun on the eternal video machine before the full impact of your righteous behavior is realized.

Because you will be serving with "all your heart, might, mind and strength," you may find fault with the bishop or other ward leaders for not being as diligent as you expect them to be. Unless it is your stewardship (which it isn't!) to correct the leaders, learn to work within the framework of the ward to introduce change. *"Don't try to magnify the bishop's calling!"* The bishop will know many things that you are not privileged to know. Many times, people (even some leaders) would say, "President, if I were you, I would do [this or that]." I would often think to myself, "If you were me and knew what I know, you would probably do exactly what I am doing." There is a reason why the saying "Every member a mission president!" is so well-known. Don't add to the problem. You become annoyed when people tell you how to serve your mission; think how the leaders must feel when a nineteen-year-old male or a twenty-one-year-old female tries to tell them how to magnify their calling.

Just as you have the potential to be the greatest talebearer in the ward, you also have the greatest potential of being the greatest peacemaker. If you use the excuse that "everybody else is doing it," you will never rise to the level to which you were foreordained. It is easy to dwell on the negative and overlook the positive. Remember, Christ is the builder. Satan is the destroyer. If what you say or do weakens and destroys, there is no question whose team you are playing on.

One of the difficult positions you may find yourself in is being in the middle of a dispute. Sometimes the opposing parties will try to attract people who agree with their philosophy. Scrupulously avoid taking sides. If you are going to be the healing agent, you must remain neutral. The Savior taught that a house divided against itself cannot stand. You will find that nine out of ten individuals can be wrong even if they all agree. What the gospel says is correct, even if it is unpopular. Teach correct principles with boldness, and leave condemnation and judgment to the Lord. To the degree you become part of the fighting among members or nonmembers, you will decrease your effectiveness as an instrument of the Lord in establishing peace. Referring to conditions that would exist just before the Second Coming, the Savior said of Zion: "It shall be the only people that shall not be at war one with another" (D&C 45:69). If we contribute in any way to the "war," we also disqualify that ward or branch from being numbered among those who are called Zion and who are thus prepared for the second coming of Christ.

If you can learn how to be in the ward without being involved in its problems, you are on your way to mastering a principle that will benefit you for the rest of your life. Is there a time for you to enter the fray? Not as a missionary! Let local leaders work to soften the hearts of the opposing parties—you focus on your assigned mission. When you speak only good about everyone you meet, the Spirit of God causes that good to be magnified. Before long these negative factors that seemed so important disappear. Make it your goal to help people achieve the unity that will qualify them as a Zion people.

28

Help for Emotions
Out of Control

A MISSION IS AN EMOTIONAL roller coaster! You will probably never experience so many highs and lows in your entire life—and all within the first month! Just when you think you can't go on, something happens and you are floating on cloud nine. You are so sure this is the beginning of a string of successes, and then boom, you hit the bottom. This is all normal. People who you thought would be investigators forever all of a sudden decide to be baptized. Your spirits soar. But a golden family you have grown to love nearly as much as your own family informs you they have decided not to be baptized. Your spirits plummet. You get transferred from the perfect area, and you're sure no other area will measure up. Your spirits drop. You receive a long-overdue letter from that special someone at home, and your spirits climb. Will it ever end? Probably not while you are serving a mission.

If you know this is going to happen, then you won't be surprised when it does. Experiencing emotional swings does not mean that you are in serious mental trouble and need professional help. It would be helpful if there were a simple gauge for measuring emotional swings so that you could tell whether what you are experiencing is normal. Unfortunately, there is no such gauge. How are you to judge whether you need help? There are two fairly reliable ways: check how other missionaries are reacting, and follow the Spirit.

By being sensitive, you will discover that everyone does not have their acts perfectly together and that you are not the only one who is struggling. One of the tactics of the adversary is to tell you that everyone else is successful and that they never have any problems. It was almost comical to listen to missionaries' expressions of unbelief when they shared the struggles they were having. It was not uncommon to hear comments like, "I can't believe you're struggling. I thought you had a handle on everything!" Or, "I thought I was the only one that felt that way. What a relief to know I'm not cracking up!" Or, "Why didn't you tell me you were having a tough time too? I thought I was the only one who was falling short of perfection." You can see how Satan tries to isolate each of us by letting us draw false conclusions. When we communicate our feelings, we soon discover that everyone goes through some rather painful growing experiences.

Often missionaries are too hard on themselves. The slightest mistake throws them into a tailspin. As it should be, we sometimes ignore the weaknesses of others and focus on our own. That brings us to the second method of evaluating our mood swings: "What does the Spirit say?" Even though we may not be perfect, we can qualify to enjoy the presence of the Spirit if we are doing *as much as the Lord expects.* That is the real key. If you're a perfectionist, you will find it nearly impossible to measure up to what you know to be right. Consider how the Lord describes those who inherit the celestial kingdom: "They shall overcome all things" (D&C 76:60). He did not say they "*have* overcome all things."

It is sometimes surprising to realize we may not be the

best judge of how well we are doing! You live so close to yourself that every weakness gets blown out of perspective. A simple demonstration will illustrate the point. Take a penny, close one eye, and hold the penny about one-half inch from the other eye. What can you see? Almost everything but the penny is blocked from view. Do you actually believe that the penny is larger than the entire world? That would be nonsense. But when viewed close up and with only one eye, it takes on giant proportions. If you put the penny on the wall and stand back ten feet, you would see how insignificant it really is. If you moved one hundred feet away, you would not be able to see the penny at all. Move ten miles away and you couldn't even see the wall! That is the way our problems are. They seem large and insurmountable when they are right on top of us. When we stand back and view them from a broader perspective, they become much more manageable.

The Spirit knows all things (see D&C 42:17). He is totally honest. If he is still with you, you are doing okay. If the Spirit is not there, you are kidding yourself to believe everything is all right. It is difficult but necessary to rely on reinforcement from above rather than from your peers. There may be a time when those around you accuse you of being out of touch with reality. These people may even be so loud and vocal that you begin to doubt yourself. That is when your ability to honestly evaluate whether the Spirit is there is essential. If the Spirit is there, your fellow missionaries, members, or others are wrong. Conversely, if everyone is telling you you're doing great but the Spirit is not there, you need to improve. Horizontal approval is only helpful while we are learning to "be taught from on high" (see D&C 43:15–16).

Sometimes when we are still learning to walk by the light

of the Spirit, we are confused and unable to determine whether we are doing all right. Consulting your companion and other missionaries may not bring the peaceful assurance that you are coping appropriately. That is the time to consult your mission president. He has seen many missionaries and has a much broader base to judge from than the missionaries. Also, he is authorized by the Lord to receive inspiration in your behalf. Be honest with him. It does absolutely no good to try to sugarcoat your condition. Tell him how you are feeling and what you are going through. Tell him what you have done to try to control your mood swings or depression. Let him counsel you. Then follow his counsel. It does no good to have the best advice in the world if you don't follow it. The counsel may not be what you want to hear; you may not even have confidence in what you are being asked to do. Do it anyway! To another unsure leader thousands of years ago, the Lord promised, "Open thy mouth, and it shall be filled, and I will give thee utterance, for all flesh is in my hands, and I will do as seemeth me good. . . . Behold my Spirit is upon you, wherefore all thy words will I justify" (Moses 6:32, 34). The president's counsel may not be the most professional you have ever heard. He probably does not have a degree in counseling psychology, but the Lord will bless his counsel, and it will work for you.

If the mission president, by the Spirit, determines that you should see a professional counselor, it does not mean that you are going crazy. It means the same thing that going to a medical doctor means. When you have a pain in your stomach, you may first begin taking certain over-the-counter medicines. If that doesn't work, then you consult a doctor. No one thinks you are weak for having an expert diagnose your sickness and prescribe medications that will help your body fight the disease. The same is true of a psychologist. If you have tried some of the standard remedies to overcome your depression or anxiety and they haven't worked, no one will call you weak for going to a professional. Because of their professional training, psychologists can often diagnose the problem and teach you coping skills to overcome the problem. That doesn't mean you don't have sufficient faith or you're not approved by Heavenly Father. It merely means you are wise enough to get the help that may enable you to continue doing the work of the Lord.

Sometimes, past events that you have been successful in suppressing come to the surface as you serve your mission. Perhaps your Heavenly Father determines that you are now strong enough to process those events so they will not come back to haunt you later. Instead of looking at the problem as a sign of weakness, try viewing it as a compliment from the Lord on your increased strength. Satan is the doctor of misdiagnosis. He will make you think you're having the flashback because you are unworthy. He was and continues to be "a liar from the beginning" (see D&C 93:25), so naturally he takes the dismal, negative point of view.

Problems can be overcome. Some very good men and women have experienced awful things. Even Abraham, the father of the faithful, had a father (Terah) who turned from his righteousness and started worshipping idols. Terah degenerated so far that he tried to kill Abraham by having the priest of Elkenah offer him as a human sacrifice (see Abraham 1). That kind of family life would certainly not be looked on as contributing in a positive way to good mental health! Abraham could have wallowed in self-pity and used that experience as an excuse for not rising to his full potential. Instead, he squared his shoulders and went on to secure for himself and his posterity all the rights of eternal family blessings.

You can do the same. Bad things that happened in the past do not mean you are a bad person or that you can't achieve all you were foreordained to do. It does mean that you must be wise enough to use all available resources to put the bad things behind you after having put them into proper perspective. A continuing dialogue with your mission president or a counselor will help you come to understand yourself better. After all, coming to know ourselves is one of the primary purposes of life. Be courageous enough to face your problems head-on. With help from above, you can and will be stronger because of your experiences. From an eternal perspective, all these struggles will seem not only natural but necessary to help us achieve our eternal destiny.

29

Your Past Sins

Long before your birth, God contemplated your role on earth. He knew when you would live, how far you would travel, and how you would fit into his eternal plan (see Deuteronomy 32:8; Acts 17:26). It is no surprise to the Almighty that you are ready to serve a mission at this very hour. He knows the mistakes you have made and the lessons you have learned the hard way. It would have been wonderful had each of us listened to and obeyed the Savior's counsel as recorded in the Sermon on the Mount: "Be ye therefore perfect, even as your Father which is in heaven is perfect" (Matthew 5:48). But we aren't perfect yet, so God provided a Savior for us. When we have repented of our past mistakes, the incomprehensible gift of the atonement of Jesus Christ makes forgiveness possible.

If you have been wise, you have learned many valuable lessons from the mistakes you made as a youth. How can you use those valuable lessons to bless others? At first you may think, "Well, I'll just tell them the pain and agony I experienced as a result of my sins, and that will help them avoid the same mistakes." That sounds good, but it is not the correct way.

Let's briefly review the repentance process and how we are to react to our past mistakes. In the Doctrine and

Covenants, the Lord presents a formula for forgiveness. "Behold, he who has repented of his sins, the same is forgiven, and I, the Lord, remember them no more. By this ye may know if a man repenteth of his sins—behold, he will confess them and forsake them" (D&C 58:42–43). Now for the formula: Confess + Forsake = God will forgive sins, and he will remember them no more.

To confess means to make a full and complete disclosure to your presiding priesthood officer if your transgression would affect your standing in the Church or your right to serve a mission. Too many missionaries attempt to cover their sins by not confessing them, only to find they cannot get the Spirit on their mission until they are clean. Remember the Lord's counsel to the early brethren in the Church: "Be ye clean that bear the vessels of the Lord" (D&C 38:42). What a surge of the Spirit comes to the burdened missionary as he allows his mission president to exercise his priesthood and lift the burden of guilt. What a blessing to yourself to become clean and receive that unmistakable witness that God has forgiven you. If you haven't completed the repentance process yet, do yourself a favor and do it now.

To forsake means to stop committing the sin both physically and mentally! It also means resolving never to commit the sin again. When one completes the repentance process by confessing and forsaking, the Lord will forgive. He also promises that he will remember the sin no more. That does not mean that you and I will forget. It doesn't even mean that our consciences won't prick us a little when we hear a discourse against that which we may have been guilty of. Why can't we completely forget? Perhaps someday we will, but for right now, one reason we remember could be to keep us from repeating the mistake. If we completely forgot the pain and embarrassment caused by our sins, what would keep us from repeating the sin in a moment of weakness?

Now an important lesson: If, after our complete repentance, God chooses to remember our sins no more, why should we insist on repeatedly bringing them up? Some unwise missionaries discuss with companions and others their past transgressions. I wonder if reminding God about our sins could possibly reinstate our guilt. I certainly am not going to take the chance! Solemnly promise not to mention again that which God has chosen to forget.

How do you use the valuable lessons you have learned to help others avoid the same mistakes? If you were to use yourself as an example, the people you are teaching (especially young people) could easily say to themselves, "Look at Elder Brown. He is such a neat guy. I want to be just like him when I grow up. If he sinned and still is as neat as he is, then it must not be too serious to commit major sins!" Can you see that they may take license from your example because they cannot see the pain and anguish you have experienced before you received a remission of your sins?

Clearly, then, you are not to recount your past sins in an effort to teach others what not to do. Instead, in teaching the principle of repentance, do as Church leaders do—illustrate your points by referring to the powerful stories of Enos (see Enos 1) and Alma the Younger (see Mosiah 27; Alma 36). Through the inspiration of the Lord, these poignant testimonials were recorded and selected for use as scripture and as such they are altogether approved of the Lord and suitable for our instruction and edification. You can best add your witness of the truth of Enos's and Alma's words not by detailing you own past sins, but by simply saying that you too know of the great inner peace and joy that are available to all through repentance. The Spirit will help your testimony find place in the hearts of your investigators.

I have watched and learned a lot from our beloved General Authorities over the years. I don't ever remember them discussing their past sins. We would do well to follow their example.

The Savior showed us how to teach without drawing negative attention to ourselves. Luke chapter 10 gives the parable of the good Samaritan. A man on the road to Jericho was attacked, beat up, robbed, and left to die by a gang of thieves. A priest and a Levite (both religious men) refused to help, but the loathsome Samaritan helped the man. The Savior got a lot of miles out of the story.

Let's see how to use the "road to Jericho" principle. Let's say the person you were before your mission was the sin-laden man on the road to Jericho. Since that time you have cleaned up your life—you have actually crucified the old man of sin and put on the new man in Christ (see Romans 6). It is the new you that people love and want to be like. Do you still remember the "old man of sin"? Sure. Can you remember how he felt, what he thought, how he suffered for his sins? Yes. Then in a teaching setting you might say, "There was once a person who made some rather serious mistakes." Without naming him, you describe the old you before you repented. More than likely those you are teaching will say to themselves, "I sure want to be like Sister Smith, but I don't want to make the stupid mistakes that other person made!" In this way you can teach others the lessons you have learned without giving your investigators license to follow your example of sin.

Far too many people have laughed with the missionaries as the missionaries recounted their past sins, only to decide they are not interested in continuing their investigation of the Church. We are to "stand as witnesses of God at *all* times and in *all* things, and in *all* places that [we] may be in, even until death" (Mosiah 18:9, emphasis added). Sharing the sinful side of your premission past diminishes you, your companion, and missionaries in general in the eyes of those who otherwise hold the missionaries in high esteem. If you have been guilty of a great sin in the past, now is a great time to resolve never to do it again either physically or mentally. Perhaps tonight in your prayers it would be appropriate to ask the Lord to forgive you again and to reinstate his promise to remember your past sins no more.

30

CHANGING FOCUS AS YOUR MISSION PROGRESSES

YOUR FIRST DAY IN THE MISSION will probably be overwhelming. There is much to do, much to learn, and many things that demand your time and attention. Your first reaction may be to throw up your hands in total frustration. The Lord gave some very good advice to the young Prophet Joseph Smith, who must have been having similar feelings: "Do not run faster or labor more than you have strength and means" (D&C 10:4). This is good advice for missionaries too. There will be people to contact, members to strengthen, talks to prepare, scriptures to memorize, lessons to master long after you have completed your mission.

Don't try to master everything at once. Take it one step at a time. You will discover soon enough that there is a necessary sequence for you to accomplish your goals. If you must learn a foreign language, you will become painfully aware that the language is a huge barrier. In frustration you may ask, "How am I to teach if I can't even speak the language?" Obviously much of your personal and companion study time should be devoted to language study. Learning a language requires relying upon the Lord so that we can become proficient enough to teach the gospel effectively.

As you begin your mission, you will need to balance lesson preparation and language study. Even if you were able to speak the language perfectly, if you don't have anything to teach, you'll have problems. The lessons provide the most concise presentation of the gospel that is available. In the MTC you got a good start at learning the first couple of discussions. You need to practice all the discussions constantly. The initial reaction of new missionaries is to spend their entire study time on the language. That will not bear the fruits you want as a missionary. The Spirit comes more readily when you are studying the gospel than when you are studying the language.

After the language and the discussions become less like obstacles and more like tools of the missionary trade, you will want to broaden your focus to include scripture study. But you need to continue to study the language and the discussions. Once the scriptures start to become sweet to you, the natural tendency is to forget everything else and focus on the scriptures. A miracle has taken place. That which you may have resisted before your mission—really getting involved in scripture study—becomes almost your top priority. Resist the temptation to focus entirely on the scriptures.

Near the midpoint of your mission, you will discover that you are now thinking in the foreign language—probably even dreaming in it. Expressing yourself fluently is rather easy. The discussions have become so familiar that you may have even been accused of giving the discussions in your sleep. At this point it would be easy to sit back and take it a little slower. Some missionaries start to "slump" in their intensity, study, and focus. However, the truly great missionaries seize the opportunity to continue to broaden their focus. They continue to study the language, lessons, and scriptures, but in addition they are now developing Christlike characteristics, studying conference addresses, and studying the gospel by topics. Discussions with these missionaries are thrilling experiences. Mere reference to a scripture, a quote, or a gospel topic elicits excitement and marvelous insights. It was always an edifying experience to be invited to participate in a district study session with the missionaries. Everyone came prepared, and we had wonderful sharing sessions; learning together, we were all edified. Those who were not as well prepared as they could have been always regretted having taken the easy way out.

Not until the very end of your mission should you begin to make plans for after your mission. Most major universities or Church schools require that you submit applications months in advance. Find out when the deadlines are and spend a single P day taking care of the details, then get back to focusing on your mission. If you have trouble with admissions to school, contact your mission president for the fastest, least distracting way to eliminate the problem. Those missionaries who talk endlessly about school, jobs, girls or guys, recreation, family, and friends lose the focus of their mission and end up wasting countless hours. Many missionaries were sorely disappointed when they reached the end of their missions and discovered they had cheated themselves of the soul-satisfying experience of looking back without regret on their service to the Lord.

CLEANLINESS—LIVING IN AN UNTIDY APARTMENT

THIS CHAPTER MAY DEAL MORE directly with you than with your companions! Let's hope you are the neat, tidy one rather than the one who is environmentally challenged. Is it important to keep your apartment clean? That seems like a fundamental question, but in the minds of many, it may not have been answered correctly.

If everyone agrees it is okay to leave clothes lying around, or dishes in the sink, or books strewn about, isn't it okay? You may have complete agreement among those living in the apartment, but you have omitted the single most important person—the Holy Ghost. When the Lord says, "Behold, mine house is a house of order, saith the Lord God, and not a house of confusion" (D&C 132:8), he means just that. A part of the Word of Wisdom that we sometimes choose to ignore because it isn't in Doctrine and Covenants 89 states, "Cease to be idle; cease to be unclean" (D&C 88:124). Assuming that you are convinced that "cleanliness is next to godliness," let's talk about some ideas of bringing order out of the chaos so common in missionary apartments.

Remember, the "honeymoon" of a companionship is the first week or so when everyone is on their best behavior. This is a critical time for establishing the rules for keeping your apartment clean. As part of your first session with your new companion, talk openly and frankly about how you want to live in the apartment. One of the biggest temptations is to treat secondary things with primary importance. By that I mean that basketball or an outing on P day is often positioned before housecleaning and laundry. In part, your success in life depends on being able to keep things in proper order. A well-planned schedule does not have to signal drudgery. If everyone agrees to spend just five minutes a day straightening up, the entire apartment can be kept orderly and odor-free.

Start with the basics: dirty clothes stink! Unless properly dried, clothes quickly mildew and give the apartment an offensive odor. Don't let moldy clothes get ahead of you. Air drying sweaty clothes will eliminate the need to do wash before the next P day. If you get hopelessly behind, get permission to wash clothes while you do some companionship study. If the clothes hamper begins to smell musty or moldy, wash it out with disinfectant.

Garments are sacred—treat them as such. It is not only poor housekeeping but poor spiritual etiquette to leave the holy garment lying around. Make sure you have a hamper or box where soiled garments can be kept until P day. After you wash them, put them in the drawer or dresser. Never compromise on handling sacred things. The Lord declared, "Trifle not with sacred things" (D&C 6:12). The word *trifle* means to treat lightly or jokingly. We cannot expect to treat disrespectfully that which God has given us and then ask for his divine help during the day.

Muddy or wet shoes should be cleaned before being put away. If left unattended, the leather will dry and crack, and your shoes will wear out faster. An inexpensive shoe tree fits inside shoes and helps them dry in the proper shape. If you have two pairs of shoes, place the shoe tree in the pair you are not using. If you rotate your shoes regularly, they will last longer and look nicer. Normal perspiration during the day will cause the leather to wear, age, and crack unless shoes are taken care of.

Suit coats and ties maintain their shape longer and look much nicer when taken off and properly hung up immediately after you return to the apartment. Nothing looks worse than a tie that has been dragged through the last three or four dinner appointments. Ties may occasionally require dry cleaning to look presentable. Dry-cleaning suit coats will prolong their usefulness. If dry cleaning is not available, you will probably not be required to wear suit coats, or you may be instructed to take those that can be washed in water. Don't wash your coat or dress if the tag specifically says to dry clean only. It will ruin the garment.

Shirts last longer if laundered weekly and kept hanging neatly in the closet when not being worn. If the collars are excessively soiled, some liquid detergent applied directly on them as you put the shirts into the washing machine helps remove stains. Recognize when your shirt has served its useful life. Use it for a rag or get rid of it. Save a few buttons before you throw the shirt away to make sure you have enough to replace missing or broken buttons on your other shirts. Consider using dental floss to sew on missing buttons—it holds much better than normal thread.

If everyone in the apartment is on the same cleanup schedule, no one will feel overly oppressed by having to do his or her job. If you agree from the start to keep a clean apartment, you can reinforce each other when you start to slip a little. Have a set time for cleaning up. The five minutes just before group prayer before you leave for the day often works well. Don't wait until five minutes before bedtime, or it won't get done. The key is to establish a routine; then follow through to make sure it happens. Left to chance, it will never work.

Doing the dishes seems to be a more difficult problem than it needs to be. If you can agree that the meal is not over until the table is cleared and the dishes done, there is no problem. Too often, as youth, we expected good old Mom to clean up after us. The trouble was, good old Mom usually *did* clean up after us! But she isn't here to clean up after you! One missionary put notes, scriptures, and reminders around the apartment to catch the eye and jog the memory of the others. Over the sink, for example, was a note that read, "It doesn't stop here! Kindly put it away!" Another clever elder wrote, "We are not here to provide a year's supply of food for the cockroaches—throw it away!" Humor is good for reminding the slothful. One note we saw on apartment inspections read, "Remember, Sister Bott will inspect tomorrow. She might be little, but she's tough!"

Clean out the refrigerator at least monthly. During one inspection, Sister Bott asked about the green stuff on the inside of the fridge. The sister said that it was probably part of the design in the porcelain. It was mold! We all laughed; a little disinfectant destroyed the design and made the place much more sanitary. If you are suffering from athlete's foot, try a little bleach in the shower to get rid of the infection. It isn't just a matter of cleanliness—your health depends on it. If you or your companion becomes ill, you both stay in the apartment, and the work doesn't get done. You cannot afford to exercise your agency in uncleanliness and hope the Lord will compensate by keeping you healthy.

Cleaning the carpet every three or four months makes the entire apartment smell better. If you wait for the next missionaries to do it, and if everybody has the same attitude, the grime and dirt will make your apartment look more like a cave or a pit than an apartment. It doesn't cost very much to rent a carpet shampoo machine from the local grocery store. If all missionaries in a district or zone shampoo their carpets on a given day, it will only cost a couple of dollars apiece, and all the apartments will be cleaned in a few hours' time. If you are called as a zone leader, you should make sure the carpets are clean in each of the apartments in the zone.

Washing the walls may not be a glorious pastime, but it sure spruces up the apartment. With just a little cleaner in a gallon of water and a couple of rags, the two of you can wash the entire apartment in a matter of minutes. The dividends are amazing. Your apartment will actually smell like home! Because not many missionaries (especially elders!) clean regularly, it may have been months or even years since the walls were washed. When the apartment looks and smells bad, it is discouraging. Do yourselves a favor and clean. If repairs need to be made, see the landlord, who is responsible to keep things working. Contact the landlord if the stove is broken, the refrigerator doesn't work, the drains are clogged, windows are broken, carpets are worn-out, or walls need painting. Normal wear and tear should not be the missionaries' responsibility. Your apartment should be clean, a fitting abode for servants of the Most High. It doesn't have to be a palace, but it shouldn't be a dump.

There is no need to live in unsanitary conditions. Doing so is hardly fitting for an ambassador of the Lord. If there needs to be an attitude adjustment, do everything within your power to help make the change. If everything else fails, ask for some suggestions from the mission president. Remember, ignoring unacceptable behavior only postpones the lesson that must be learned. Eventually we must learn to be clean enough to be welcomed into the presence of God. We aren't doing anyone a favor if we hope someone else will help our companion learn to be clean. Some future spouse will be thankful that his or her mate has learned the skills of cleanliness.

32

If Your Companion
Is Disobedient

ONE OF THE GREAT CHALLENGES you may face as a missionary is dealing with companions or other missionaries who are selectively obedient. They probably had the burning desire to be perfect missionaries when they first arrived, but found it more difficult than they had anticipated. It may have been that everyone else in their apartment was sleeping in a little when they first arrived, so rather than fight it, they just joined. At first it didn't seem like such a big deal; nobody apostatized over it. Then maybe their companions didn't make it out of their apartments on time or stayed out a little late a few times. It isn't that serious, they rationalize. Everyone else is doing it. Before long, obedience to any rule becomes less and less important, and it becomes easier and easier to rationalize. When you arrive on the scene, things may be way out of hand. What can you do? Perhaps a short story will give you some ideas.

When I was a teenager, all the guys would congregate on the large lawn—a perfect football field—alongside my house. My mother, however, had planted fruit trees along each side and down the middle of the lawn. An orchard had serious drawbacks as far as a football field was concerned, so we systematically disposed of the row of trees in the middle of our football field. Through careful neglect, all of them died except one. It was about on the twenty-yard line. We tried everything we could think of to kill the tree without being too conspicuous. We kept the water from getting to it, we broke off several limbs, and we even tried to ring the bark so it would die a "normal" death. Nothing worked. From pure meanness, the tree grew to about shoulder height. Then the main trunk took a ninety-degree angle, grew for about eighteen inches, then continued to grow upwards. We called it "the Devil Tree."

Over the years we had learned to play around the Devil Tree, so it wasn't that big of a deal. One evening a rather large group of us were playing football. My brother was the best quarterback, so everybody wanted to play on his team. I was usually on the opposing team, but not this evening. It was nearing the time we needed to quit for the evening, but because we were tied, we decided that whoever scored next would be the winner.

After a short huddle we decided on a pass play. The more likely pass receivers were to run crisscross patterns, and I was to break straight down the field for the bomb. As I approached the Devil Tree, I was to look over my shoulder, catch the ball, duck under the horizontal branch, and race for the goal line. The Devil Tree was to act as pass interference for those would-be tacklers.

Everything went according to plan. The crisscross pattern confused our opponents. No one really believed I would be the primary receiver, so I went unguarded down the field. I looked over my shoulder and caught the perfect spiral pass. Then came the problem: the devil had moved the tree ten yards closer than I had calculated. As I turned around to head down the field, the horizontal branch caught me right in the throat. I fell to the ground, waiting for the death I knew was going to come any moment. I couldn't breathe or swallow. The entire group gathered around me. When I didn't die, they did the only thing a manly football team could do—they dragged me off the field so they could continue the game. I finally decided I would go into the house and see if I would ever be able to swallow again or whether I would slowly starve to death. To my amazement I could swallow. I decided to return to the game.

When I went outside I was shocked. It was pitch black. The guys on the field called for me to join them. I argued that it was too dark; we'd have to finish the game the next day. They again gathered around me, everyone arguing at the top of their lungs that there was plenty of light to finish the game.

For once I had a bright idea. I agreed to play but invited them to take a short break to have some punch. They agreed. We raced for the house. When we came back outside, to everyone's utter amazement it was totally dark! So they agreed we should quit for the night and continue the game the next night. So goes the story; now for its application.

The sunlight had dimmed so slowly that no one on the field realized it was getting darker. It was not until they were brought into the light that they realized how "in the dark" they had been. You should be way ahead of me by this time.

If you give into the temptation to join the other missionaries in their disobedience, you will slowly lose the light of the Holy Ghost, just as they have. If you can get them into the light, convincing them they are in the dark is easy. How do you get a person into the light? Think of the times when you enjoy the greatest amount of the Spirit—when you are teaching a discussion, studying the scriptures, praying, discussing a gospel subject, serving other people, or maybe sitting in a zone conference.

First determine if there is anyone to help you get the Spirit back. Often others feel uncomfortable with how things are going, but they are not bold enough to stand up. These individuals will gladly join you. If you can get just one other person to join with you in obedience, the rest will start to sense the condition they are in and slowly join you. I have witnessed over and over again the power of the one. Maybe you can't change the entire world—but maybe you can! It usually doesn't do any good to point the finger of condemnation at others. A more effective way to help others change is to turn up the light in your own life and let them see how dark their light has become.

You may think you are going to take some flak. You might. But again, the promise of the Lord is sure: "You should not have feared man more than God. Although men set at naught the counsels of God, and despise his words— yet you should have been faithful; and he would have extended his arm and supported you against all the fiery darts of the adversary; and he would have been with you in every time of trouble" (D&C 3:7–8). Remember, your companion has made the same commitment to obey that you did. You are not trying to get your companion to do something he or she hasn't already promised the Lord. You are just trying to help your companion stand without shame before the Eternal Judge. Reread the chapter on using the "honeymoon" of your companionship to establish your game plan. But remember the way your companion serves his or her mission has a direct impact on how successful you are in serving your mission. You cannot afford to ignore the attitude and hope the president will soon transfer one of you. It may be three or four months before you are separated. That could mean a waste of an eighth to a sixth or more of your mission. Three companions like that could destroy half of your mission. You must determine to get things going with your very first companion.

If you have tried everything you can think of to motivate the disobedient companion and nothing has worked, try involving your leaders—the district leader, the zone leader, the assistants. If that doesn't work, call the mission president. Explain the problem and what you have done to remedy it. Ask if he has additional suggestions. Generally, if your companion is having a problem that severe, he or she has had it for a long time. Very seldom does a missionary go from being involved, dedicated, and enthusiastic to being lazy and disobedient. The president may know tactics that have worked with other missionaries.

After you have consulted with the president, don't be too insistent that one of you be transferred. The Lord may have some valuable lessons in mind for you. If you insist on being transferred, you may not have learned the necessary lessons to succeed in future callings. I thought the Lord had abandoned me when I received a companion who was less than motivated. I was there to work and couldn't see the value of being saddled with a lazy companion. We didn't have phones, so I couldn't call the president and demand a transfer. I tried to make the best of the situation and actually became good friends with this elder. After a few months he was transferred. From then on I was in the driver's seat. The missionaries worked at my pace because I was the senior companion. Years later, when I was called to preside over a mission myself, I realized how valuable the lessons in motivating people were that I had learned from my lazy companion. Now I thank the Lord for teaching me those lessons that I would use repeatedly a quarter of a century later.

Now for some advice on what not to do. Don't join your companion in disobedience. You may be called a "nark" or a "rat" or be made to feel guilty for informing the mission president that your companion is disobedient. Sometimes it is worthwhile to save your companion from himself, such as when he tells you, "Elder, I'm going out alone for a couple of hours. You stay here and answer the phone." Nine times out of ten he will be planning to meet a girl. Your answer should be definite and in the form of a promise rather than a threat. "The minute you walk out that door alone, I will call the president," or "Why don't I call the president. You can tell him what your plans are so I won't get in trouble for letting you out of my sight." That is always a show-stopper! If he threatens to beat you up or whatever, so be it. Better that he beat you up and you save his soul than you cower in the shadows while he commits spiritual suicide.

Your companion needs to know right up front that you plan to be obedient and that you expect him also to honor his commitment to obey the mission rules. Of course, not every companion will be disobedient. Most of your companions will be great, obedient people. But if you should get one who is not yet converted, it is nice to know what to do.

The adversary is very powerful and constantly tries to destroy you and your companion, so you must be very definite about how you plan to thwart Satan's plans. In every case in which serious transgressions occur, the transgressor's companion was either asleep or too timid to say anything about the obviously wrong behavior. In every case when the disobedient companion was sent home, the companion who stayed behind felt terrible for not speaking out earlier. Don't find yourself looking at your mission with regret. With a little humor and a lot of seriousness, you can ensure that Satan never makes any inroads into your companionship.

33

·········

PRACTICING SKILLS FOR A SUCCESSFUL MARRIAGE

EVERYTHING YOU DO IN LIFE prepares you for what is coming next. You can get a running head start on marriage if you will identify and master the principles that are common to both missions and marriage. In the mission the two "M" words go hand in hand—mission and marriage. Missions and marriage share many characteristics.

There are two of you in the companionship. You are called on to live together for a set amount of time. You are required to communicate, solve problems, negotiate, compromise, exercise self-control, and work toward common goals. Your ways of thinking will be different. Your backgrounds will be different. You may both be hardheaded or unassertive. You will both have habits that will annoy the other. You will have to work to be on the same team and not to compete against each other. You will have good days and dog days. You will be tempted to point out your companion's faults. You will become attached to each other and probably shed tears when you are to be separated.

You will probably pray to be blessed with super companions. Every once in a while the president will give you one, just to show you how great it is to be equally yoked to someone who is willing and able to match strides with you. But more commonly you'll get a companion you have to motivate. If you remember how tiring it is to always have to motivate someone, it will be easier as you begin to look for an eternal companion. You may have a companion who has more energy than you. Think how it would be to be married to someone who is constantly pulling you along and trying to get you more involved. It isn't that one energy level is better than another—you just need to realize what can happen if you are not careful in choosing a marriage partner. Being equally yoked in marriage leads to peace, harmony, and mutual progress. Being unequally yoked results in frustration, tension, and disharmony.

If you are a clean person, then you will be frustrated by those who are more casual in their approach to housework. Note where you are when it comes to cleanliness. One time we went to inspect the apartment of two elders who were both pretty casual about housecleaning. The clothes were stacked up on the bed, on the floor, and on the table—anywhere there was a little space. But they were both proud; in their eyes they had done a good job in getting ready for the inspection. After we left, we looked at each other and wondered aloud what kind of women would tolerate those two characters. They were good missionaries but definitely not very tidy.

Learning to deal with differences will make your transition into marriage a lot easier. If you don't learn how to compromise, you will have a difficult time in marriage. It is easy to call the president and demand a change when you get a challenging companion. But that would probably be one of the worst mistakes you could make. In working with missionaries who differ greatly from their companions, I have noticed a definite lack of creativity in solving problems. Given a particular problem (like unwashed dishes), I asked missionaries to list as many solutions to the problem as they could. At first they would come up with one or two solutions; almost always the first solution was to have the companion change. When I refused to accept that, they would usually come up with four or five other possibilities. When we brainstormed together, we could usually come up with ten or twelve solutions. Get in the habit of finding creative solutions. When problem solving becomes a game, it is fun and exciting. If you look at problems as indications of failure or fault, then problem solving is drudgery.

As I met with missionaries who were struggling with companions, areas, members, nonmembers, or life in general, I found that they were reluctant to look for the positive. If you think of the thousands of dollars and countless hours you spend to obtain a college education, doesn't it seem reasonable that something as important as eternal marriage and eternal families would require at least as much effort? It is possible to make the celestial kingdom without a college education, but it is not possible to make the highest degree of the celestial kingdom without a successful marriage and family life. Now is definitely the time to learn.

If you think everything you learn must be positive, you will limit yourself. You can learn from some companions those things that you do not ever want to have in your marriage! Identifying the traits you don't want can be as important as identifying those you do want. For example, you may have a companion who is never on time. That could drive you up the wall. So in selecting an eternal companion, you will prefer someone who, in addition to having other good qualities, is as punctual as you are. The opposite is also true.

If you are more casual in your approach to punctuality, being married to a time-conscious fanatic will give you fits until you change, because the likelihood that your spouse will change is not very good.

If I had my first mission to do over again, I would begin by making two lists in the very back of my journal. One list would be entitled "Traits that are a *must* in my marriage partner." The second list would be entitled "Traits to avoid in selecting my eternal companion." If you can approach each companionship as a blessing to help you prepare for marriage, you will be better able to endure certain companions and situations. Of course, you don't have to learn the lessons of life with these companions who are expendable. You can wait and learn them with your nonexpendable eternal companion. The price you pay if you wait to learn crucial lessons is much higher than you would pay while on your mission. In the mission, you're only with each companion for a few short months, but it is hoped that in marriage you will not be changing eternal companions.

It is equally important to identify how people react to you. You may have been rather insensitive as a youth, not really caring whether you were obnoxious. Your awareness of the feelings of others may not have been one of your strengths. Now is the time to work on this. It is painful to realize how far you have to go when some of these things begin to dawn on you.

How do you become more sensitive? Start watching the reactions of those around you. When you act a certain way, they may raise their eyebrows. They may furrow their brows at some of your actions. Listen to what people are saying *about* you, not *to* you. They will usually speak just loud enough for you to hear even if they're speaking to someone else. Unfortunately, only a few people are both honest and bold enough to tell you directly how you come across. It would be well to find at least one person like this. However, it isn't helpful to always ask someone else how you can improve. That becomes old. It is far better to develop that kind of relationship with your Heavenly Father. He can inspire you to change those characteristics that are counterproductive in your personality.

As you are blessed with leadership and other responsibilities, you may find that your opinion becomes very valuable—in your own eyes. Resist the urge to fix every problem or to counsel others on how to solve their problems. As you focus more on being an example, you may find that the need to expound the eternal truths you have learned diminishes. Ask yourself a serious question: "If I were the only standard works others had read and they were to follow my example perfectly, how Christlike would they be?" The closer we come to living up to our potential, the easier it is to see the good in others and overlook their weaknesses. People respond much more readily to positive reinforcement than to criticism. If you can put that concept into practice, you will be much better prepared for marriage.

As you lose yourself in helping and building others, you will find that your whole soul enlarges. As you come unto Christ and help others do the same, everyone is uplifted. When you become selfish and demanding, you begin to shrivel and atrophy. Love and helpfulness are strange commodities: the more you give them away, the more you have! That's what marriages and families thrive on—losing yourself to help your spouse and children. If you demand an equal relationship, you will be setting the stage for conflict and problems in marriage. If your only desire is to make your companion successful, you will find that he or she will do the same for you. What a fabulous key for marriage. If you expect a fifty-fifty relationship and one of you falls just one point short, there will be a gap in your marriage. However, if you give 100 percent for your spouse and he or she does the same for you, if either or both of you fall a little short, no problem—you are still adequately covered. A mission is a great opportunity to perfect this kind of unselfish behavior.

Although you should not focus on or daydream about your future marriage, you will be wise to begin a list of qualities that you desire in a companion. You will never have another opportunity to be welcomed into so many different homes to observe firsthand how marriage and family life works. Be an observer. Take mental notes in every home you enter. Watch for the positive and note the negative. Determine what you would do differently if you were in the same position, but do not try to tell others how to be successful in marriage. When I was a missionary, I heard a wise man say, "Before I was married, I was an expert in both marriage and child rearing. Then I got married and was only an expert in child rearing. Once the children came, I joined the rest of the married couples—parents who were trying to do the best they knew how!" I liked that counsel then, and I am convinced that it was correct; my wife and I are now just trying to do the best we know how in raising our kids.

34
....

DEALING WITH THOSE WHO
TEASE ABOUT GOING HOME

ONE OF THE IRONIES OF A MISSION is that sometimes the very
people who are there to help you succeed seem to be those
who cause you to stumble. So it goes as you approach the
end of your full-time service. By this time in your mission
you will realize that eighteen months or two years is not
going to last forever. Your time is rapidly running out, and
you want to make the best of it. You try to shut out all
thoughts of home, schooling, marriage, jobs, and postmission life. Just when you have decided to be totally focused,
the harassment from other missionaries and members starts.

It is generally done innocently—and because others
don't know what else to say. Nevertheless, it is unwelcome.
The missionaries who have only been out for a few months
may look at you enviously, especially if they are in the homesick stage. They may make comments like, "You lucky dog. I
wish I were going home instead of you!" At that point you
may want to trade places with them. Of course, that isn't
possible. But you can help them by saying something like, "It
seems like only yesterday I was in your position and thought
my mission would never end. Tomorrow you'll be on your
way home, so make every minute count." Some of the flak

will come from missionaries who have been out long enough to know better. Their time is also drawing short. They may tease you because they realize their days are numbered too. Comments such as, "I'm sure glad it's you going home and not me!" are common. If you have served the way you should, your answer can reflect some teaching. "I'm glad I took advantage of the opportunities as they came along. I'd hate to be where I am and have a lot of regrets. If I were so lucky to be in your position, I would redouble my efforts to make sure I ended positively."

Members constitute a different problem. They have become accustomed to missionaries coming and going. But that doesn't make it any easier for them to say good-bye. If you have served with honor, they will have grown to love you like a son or daughter. They are a bit more realistic. The chances of your coming back to visit very often are slim. Therefore, when they say farewell, they are cutting the ties for the rest of mortality. Often they are uncomfortable with showing too much emotion, because it makes things harder. So instead they joke and tease you. If they are sensitive, the joking will be in good taste. If they haven't had much experience, the teasing could be a bit more cruel. Often you will hear comments such as, "Oh, you'll just go home and forget all about us. You really don't care about us anyway!" That hurts because it's not true. Try to help them understand. You might say something like, "It is true our paths may not cross again, but one of the most consoling parts of the gospel is the knowledge that we will be together again in the celestial kingdom, where we never need to say good-bye again." This reassures members and gives them hope that the joy you have shared together in the gospel will not be lost forever.

People tend to joke and laugh when they are rather

uncomfortable and don't know what else to do. If you promise to keep in touch, then do so. Avoid making too many promises. Life at home will be busy and challenging enough to demand your full attention. Even the best intentions to visit or write or call may not be reasonable. The problem comes when you promise and do not fulfill your promise. That casts a poor light on you as an individual and on missionaries as a whole. It would be better to be more conservative in making promises. Then if you have the time and inclination to keep in touch, it will come as a pleasant surprise. If you find you can't keep in touch, there will be no promises broken and no confidences destroyed.

Missions are like other phases in your life. You write each page of a chapter one day at a time. When the chapter is complete, although you reread it occasionally, other chapters demand your complete attention. Those missionaries who never quite leave the mission are not viewed as well-balanced individuals. Just as you may have hated to see your high school experience come to a close, so you may hate to see your mission experience end. But just as you discovered that there was life after high school, so you will also discover that there is a wonderful life after your mission.

A final observation about leaving your mission: strengthen those around you. You have worked hard to help those good people, whether members or nonmembers, and the last thing you want to hear is that they have wandered off into forbidden paths. If you made any commitments, honor them before you leave. Don't leave any unpaid bills. Bad feelings are created if you don't pay for what you receive. If you have promised to present a fireside for the young men and young women of the ward, schedule it before the crunch of the last few weeks hits. If you have promised to look up a relative or friend who lives in your area, now is the time to do it. If you have promised to do a service project with other members of your district or zone, schedule it before the last minute. One thing is for sure—the last few weeks will be so busy and hectic that you will wonder if somebody has sped up the clock. If you consciously start about three months before your departure date to organize the things you want to do before you leave, your departure will be a lot less hectic. If you fail to take this advice, you will know firsthand what I refer to—your mission will end in chaos.

Even though others may tease you, don't respond bitterly or angrily. Someday you will be glad that you didn't stoop to their level but instead tried to maintain a Christlike attitude during those difficult and trying days. You can do it, but it will require constant, diligent effort.

"NINETY-NINE YARDS DOTH NOT A TOUCHDOWN MAKE"

MANY FOOTBALL GAMES HAVE been lost because the team with the ball has been stopped on the one-yard line. It seems that my high school team suffered more than our share of that kind of defeat. Usually we had played the entire game valiantly, only to find ourselves from one to six points behind as the final minutes of the fourth quarter ticked away. With all the spirit and enthusiasm we could muster, we would start down the field. Short gains from running plays combined with larger gains from well-executed pass plays brought us within striking distance of the goal line. Then came the plague. It was usually a do-or-die situation. A field goal would only tie the game, or we needed at least six points to win. Now the gamble. Did we go for the win, or settle for a tie? Being eternal optimists, we always went for the win. We would be on the one-yard line, with only time enough to execute one more play. The coach would give us the sign to go for the win! The snap of the ball, the crashing of pads and helmets, and the preliminary signals by our players of a touchdown were followed by disappointment when we discovered we were still on the one-yard line.

I watched with sorrow and disappointment both as a

young missionary and years later as a mission president when young men and young women served valiantly, only to let up at the end. In fact, we would do well to analyze and discard the phrase "the bump, the hump, the slump, and the dump." "The bump" is the six-month mark for an elder. He has been able to rely on his trainer and senior companion to carry most of the load up to that point. He now needs to bump it in gear and start carrying his share of the load. "The hump" is the midway point. Missionary work is not new to him. He knows how to teach, contact, commit, and be successful. "The slump" is where the terminology begins to break down. That is the eighteen-month mark for elders. Right when they are the most effective, some tend to go into a slump. The word itself sounds negative and defeated. The ending sounds even worse: "dump." That sounds like something you do to garbage! I mention elders because the terminology was not common among the sisters. Being older and somewhat more focused, they seldom exhibited this syndrome.

Perhaps if you need to use some words to describe *your* mission, you should say, "Bump, Hump, Pump, and Jump." The first two we have already talked about. In track events, the last leg of the race is the time to really "kick." That final burst of effort often wins the race. The runner is tired and his muscles need some rest, but the winner knows the glory is worth the sacrifice. So it is with missionary work. At the eighteen-month mark, your skills should be finely developed. If you have had to learn a foreign language, you are better than you have ever been. You are usually proficient enough in your own area that you are given the added responsibility of leadership. Perhaps the word "pump" can indicate an infusion of energy, effort, diligence, and hard work into your routine that will carry you to victory. Yes, you are tired. Missionary work is extremely demanding—physically, mentally, and spiritually. What a compliment you pay to your future spouse and children to have finished on the run the most difficult task that God has ever given his young sons and daughters to this point in your lives. You may feel that all you have left to do is "dump" at the end of your service. You will find, however, that the Lord will literally energize you in every way as you "jump" into the next exciting chapter of your life.

At the end of your mission, you will look back at what you have accomplished. If you end on a high, all you see is a strong finish and the high points of your mission. On the other hand, if you finish on a slump, you will look back with regret and see all the things you wished you had done or that you wished you hadn't! Too many times as we took missionaries to the airport for their return home, one or more of them would be in tears. Often they asked, "President, what can I do to make up for the mistakes I've made on my mission?" Frequently the only answer I could give was, "Well, it's a little late to worry about that. There is your final boarding call. Now go home, pick up the pieces, and do the very best you can with the rest of your life." My heart ached for them. Earlier efforts had been made to let them know that this day would come, and they would deeply regret the time they had wasted. Usually the warnings fell on deaf ears. They would act as if they'd heard it all before, and they knew what they were doing.

Another advantage of ending strong is momentum. The direction and the rate of improvement you establish on your mission will seldom be exceeded by what you do in the future. If you serve casually in the mission, it would take a major miracle to increase your rate of perfecting yourself once you are on your own and you no longer have the support system to help remind you of your commitment to perfection. If, on the other hand, you end strong, greatly increasing in righteousness, you will likely continue on until you reach perfection. I am confident that the leaders of the Church were young missionaries who diligently tried to serve with "all their heart, might, mind and strength." Join their circle by serving well.

It would be less than honest to claim that sustaining a winning pace until you leave the mission field is going to be easy. On the contrary, it will be very difficult. There seems to be a built-in resistance to continued diligence. Those missionaries who are overcome with the irresistible urge to slack off claim that it is impossible to surge ahead to the very end.

After serving for six months as a mission president, I asked the zone leaders to list the missionaries who had ended their mission on the run. To their surprise and my disappointment, they could only agree on one name. They all agreed that in order to do it, this young man had taken a lot of flak from the other missionaries. They had teased him, called him names, and tried to lure him off the track by using every tactic they could think of—all because he was doing what they knew they should be doing but didn't have the dedication to do. I told them in that meeting: "Elders, this cannot be. You are better men than that. You have earned the right to be numbered among the elect who are considered potential leaders in God's earthly kingdom. Will you renew your commitment to finish honorably?" They all consented. Six months later, I again asked the zone leaders to list those who had finished valiantly. To my satisfaction, their response was, "President, we can't do that. It seems to us that all the missionaries are working right up to the end!" That is more what we are capable of.

It may be the thing in your mission to slump off at the end. If it is, be ready for the opposition as you serve faithfully. How do you do it? Simple. Just serve one day at a time as though it were your last day. Serve so that you can look back each night without regret. If you have to, you can promise yourself that you'll relax tomorrow. Of course, when "tomorrow" comes, it is "today"! Then you keep promising yourself that "tomorrow" you will relax, but thankfully, tomorrow never comes. Relatively few will taste the sweetness of the fruit of a 100 percent mission. Why don't you add your name to the list?

If you find yourself falling short of that goal, renew your commitment. It is better to serve the last few months on the dead run than not to serve at all with valor. One young man whom I had worked with for his entire mission had chosen to take a casual approach to serving. He was "cool" and didn't want to be labeled as a hardworking missionary. I warned him in every interview that he would regret it.

Early one morning I received a telephone call from this elder. He wanted an immediate interview. I feared he had broken some mission rule that would necessitate his being sent home. He was then serving one hundred miles from the mission headquarters. I told him I would be there as soon as I could. I prayed hard all the way there that my fears would not be confirmed. To my joy, my fears were ungrounded. It seems that the night before, he and his companion had come home early because an appointment had been canceled. They were playing cards when the other two elders who shared their apartment arrived. One elder flopped down in the chair, kicked off his shoes, and exclaimed, "I have never been so tired in my whole life. I have never felt better in my whole life. I wouldn't trade missionary work for anything!"

The Spirit just happened to bother my casual friend. He told me that he stayed up all night thinking about the tired elder's statement. He said, "I want to feel that way about my mission. Unless I change and change fast, I will never know what he was talking about. President, what must I do to change?"

That was the best question he could have asked. We spent a couple of hours outlining what he had to do. Aided by the Spirit, both he and I learned a great deal. That hundred-mile trip home was the most pleasant of my entire mission. To my discredit, I doubted he had the mettle to follow through with the course we outlined for him. To my amazement, he did! He ended on an all-time high. According to his testimony the night before he left the mission, his last six months were the greatest he had ever experienced. He said he was bone tired and had never felt better. His only regret is that he didn't serve his entire mission like that. I have great expectations for that elder. His momentum and direction will carry him far in the Church and in life.

Consider for a moment what difference it would have made to us if the Savior had slacked off his last week! No Atonement, no Crucifixion, no Resurrection, no possibility of eternal life for us. Aren't we glad he worked right up to the very last?

I have wondered several times over the past twenty-five years what difference it would have made in the lives of those who were on my football team if we had been able to successfully cover that final yard. I wonder often what would happen if every missionary would work hard right up to the last day. How much sooner could we succeed in converting the world? Remember, "ninety-nine yards doth not a touchdown make." Go for the score!

36

WRITING YOURSELF A LETTER

TOWARD THE VERY END OF your mission, you may begin to worry a little about going home. Will you be able to keep the Spirit the way you did while serving your mission? Will you fall off the table spiritually, as you have seen some returned missionaries do? Will you be able to fit in without compromising your standards? Dozens of other questions flood your mind. What can you do to make it through those first few months at home?

When I was about to complete my first mission, I was cleaning out my desk in the mission office when I noticed my old manual typewriter. Without really thinking about what I was doing, I took a piece of mission letterhead and put it into the typewriter. I started to type: "Dear Elder Bott . . . " I went on to explain to myself that I had now successfully completed the most difficult assignment that the Lord had ever given me. I reminded myself of the commitment I had made to continue faithful.

The next paragraph started a series of questions. "Are you studying the scriptures daily? Do you attend all your meetings? Are you a full tithe payer? Are you keeping your thoughts clean as you promised you would? Are your relationships with members of the opposite sex on a plane as high as you said they would be? Are you being kind to your brother and sisters?" The list continued as I thought through every phase of my life and the commitments I had made.

I realized I was still very much under the influence of my call as a missionary. I concluded the two-page, single-spaced letter with the following admonition: "Now Elder Bott, if you have slipped in any of these areas, repent. Your eternal life depends on it! Your Friend, Elder Bott." Then I sealed it, postdated it for six months later, and put it with the other papers I was sending home.

A couple months later, I was sorting through my mission papers and ran across the letter. Although it hadn't yet been six months, I decided to open it and read what I had written. As I read through the long list of questions, I felt a flood of memories, emotions, and a little guilt. In answer to most of the questions, I could honestly report that I was doing well. But a couple caused me to sit up and take notice. When I got to the end and read my rather pointed challenge to either shape up or perish, I couldn't really get mad at anybody, because it was I who had written the letter!

I put the letter on my dresser by my bed and read it at least once a week for the next three months or so until I lost it. But I discovered it had helped me through the turbulent times of readjustment. As a mission president, I suggested to the returning missionaries that they do something like that. Many followed the counsel and later reported that the letter had greatly helped them keep one eye focused on things of eternal worth.

You may think it is a dumb idea, but it worked for me and has worked for many others. If you decide not to write a letter, at least take the advice of another mission president who suggested that "every Sunday for the first three months, and then monthly for the rest of your life, hold a personal interview with yourself. Ask yourself seriously and soberly how you are doing with regard to your activity in the Church, your attitude, your obedience level, and your spiritual state of health."

If you can maintain your obedience and spirituality for the first six months after your return, you will probably stay active for the rest of your life. There is a little psychology in the letter or the interview. If someone else chastises you for not being as righteous as you know you should be, it is natural for you to become defensive. If, however, you are the one chewing yourself out, whom are you going to get mad at?

The main point is to have some definite, clearly defined method of coping during those first few months. You may have heard of more creative or more effective methods. Don't leave your level of righteousness to chance. If you have firmly decided to keep active and keep the Spirit with you, you will find it isn't that difficult. If you haven't decided, it is far too easy to discontinue those practices that brought the Spirit into your life while you served your mission. Remember that prayer, scripture study, and service brought the Spirit back in a hurry. Those same three things will continue to bring the Spirit into your life as a returned missionary.

37

EARNING THE PROMISED
REWARDS

SOME MARVELOUS REWARDS HAVE been promised by the Lord
to those who "fail not to continue faithful in all things"
(D&C 84:80). These rewards are available to every missionary who is willing to pay the price; they are not automatic.

Far too many young men and women have the mistaken
idea that just being in the mission field for eighteen or
twenty-four months constitutes serving an honorable mission. Anyone can be away from home for two years, but only
the diligent can serve an honorable mission. This entire book
has been dedicated to offering advice to help you diligently
serve a mission. If you distinguish yourself as an outstanding missionary, what is in it for you?

The great missionary section, Doctrine and Covenants 4,
promises that whosoever "thrusteth in his sickle with his
might, the same layeth up in store that he perisheth not, but
bringeth salvation to his soul" (D&C 4:4). Not bad for
starters: you will not perish, and you will bring salvation to
your soul. If you have served with the Christlike characteristics listed in Doctrine and Covenants 4, you are well on your
way to making those characteristics part of you. You have
developed faith—for without faith it is impossible to please

God (see Hebrews 11:6). You have learned to have hope in Christ and his infinite atonement and hope in your ability to live the gospel well enough to qualify to participate in the great events incident to the Second Coming. You have also developed a hope that through continued obedience, you can qualify for exaltation in the celestial kingdom. As you have forgotten yourself, you find yourself loving more intensely those you are serving. All thoughts of personal comfort and convenience are gone. You focus on helping your beloved investigators, even if it costs you a great deal personally. This unselfish love is charity. The overwhelming gratitude you feel for having been chosen to aid the Savior in "bring[ing] to pass the immortality and eternal life of man" (Moses 1:39) helps you realize that your love of God increases as you serve him. That love enriches everyone you meet. You no longer have a self-serving attitude or a desire to embarrass or hurt anyone; your whole life and attitude have changed as you have learned to love. You have learned how to focus on spiritual things. Bringing souls to Christ is more important to you than food and drink. A sense of urgency has helped you through the tough times. Time becomes a valuable commodity that just seems to slip away. These five characteristics were necessary just to qualify you for the work.

The characteristics that separate the outstanding missionaries from those who are just "there" are found in Doctrine and Covenants 4:6. The Lord urges us to constantly remember faith, virtue, knowledge, temperance, patience, brotherly kindness, godliness, charity, humility, and diligence. As you focus on these qualities during your eighteen months or two years of your mission, you will notice that it is easier to get answers to prayers, to feel the Spirit with you constantly, to be more tolerant of those who are struggling, and to be more positive in the face of overwhelming odds. In fact, the characteristics listed in Doctrine and Covenants 4:6 sound very much like those outlined by Peter in 2 Peter 1:1–10 as prerequisite to making your calling and election sure. I don't think that the similarities in the lists are coincidental. You will be doing for eighteen months or two years what Christ did during his ministry. His reward was exaltation. Why should yours be any less?

You may feel that your past has caused you to start a mission with two strikes against you. Maybe that is why the Lord revealed through the Prophet Joseph Smith that "nevertheless, ye are blessed, for the testimony which ye have borne is recorded in heaven for the angels to look upon; and they rejoice over you, and *your sins are forgiven you*" (D&C 62:3; emphasis added). What a reward for faithfully bearing your testimony to members, nonmembers, and other missionaries.

Thomas B. Marsh, an early missionary for the Church, experienced his share of problems with his family, as the Lord indicated: "Behold, you have had many afflictions because of your family" (D&C 31:2). Later in that same section the Lord gives a promise that is applicable to us as well: "Therefore, thrust in your sickle with all your soul, and your sins are forgiven you, and you shall be laden with sheaves upon your back, for the laborer is worthy of his hire. Wherefore, your family shall live" (verse 5). Put the Lord to the test and see if he does not bless and prosper your family for your diligent service. Let him bless them in his own time and in his own way and according to his own will (see D&C 88:68).

You may serve under less-than-ideal circumstances. In fact, just getting a good meal or a decent shower or place to sleep may be a near impossibility. At times you may think a mission is too great of a sacrifice to make. Again, you should remember what the Lord revealed through the Prophet: "Behold, I have seen your sacrifices, and will forgive all your sins; I have seen your sacrifices in obedience to that which I have told you. Go, therefore, and I make a way for your escape, as I accepted the offering of Abraham of his son Isaac" (D&C 132:50). What are you willing to do to ensure that past transgressions are eternally erased from your record?

The Lord promised faithful missionaries: "Any man that shall go and preach this gospel of the kingdom, and fail not to continue faithful in all things, shall not be weary in mind, neither darkened, neither in body, limb, nor joint; and a hair of his head shall not fall to the ground unnoticed. And they shall not go hungry, neither athirst" (D&C 84:80). Think of it! If you serve faithfully, you will not be weary in mind—you may be dog tired, but your mind will be clear and alert. You will not be darkened in mind, body, limb, or joint. Satan will not have control over your mind or body. He may work you over a little, but he will not have power to permanently slow you down. For some of you elders, the next part may have a great amount of appeal: "a hair of his head shall not fall to the ground unnoticed." Because missions come at a critical time when some young men lose a lot of hair, you can be comforted that heaven has given you a great deal of notice! I presume the intent of this phrase is to show how closely attended we are by unseen beings who are eager and willing to help whenever needed. In fact, a little later in the same section, the Lord promises: "Whoso receiveth you, there I will be also, for I will go before your face. I will be on your right hand and on your left, and my Spirit shall be in your hearts, and mine angels round about you, to bear you up" (D&C

84:88). Think of having the Savior constantly near you and angels around to bear you up and keep you going. Not bad company for the diligent missionary!

The opposition you will face as a diligent servant of the Lord would make the normal young man or woman cower in fear. You will have a notable absence of fear because the Lord has promised, "Verily, thus saith the Lord unto you— there is no weapon that is formed against you shall prosper" (D&C 71:9). Of course, that does not excuse you from using common sense and avoiding dangerous situations. But it does mean that when you have done all you can do, divine help will protect you until your work on the earth is finished.

Promises made to faithful missionaries are not limited to the Doctrine and Covenants. In Mark 10:28–30, the Apostle Peter asks what's in it for missionaries who have given up everything for missionary service. The Savior's answer is sure and unwavering: "Verily I say unto you, There is no man that hath left house, or brethren, or sisters, or father, or mother, or wife, or children, or lands, for my sake, and the gospel's, but he shall receive an hundredfold now in this time, houses, and brethren, and sisters, and mothers, and children, and lands, with persecutions; and in the world to come eternal life." You can see what tremendous blessings are promised to those who serve the Lord faithfully not only for eighteen months or two years but also ever after—they receive the divine promise that their lives will be enriched one hundred times over.

On your mission you will learn the great lessons of life. That is a given. But the price tag for learning is much lower in the mission than when you are actually married. Since, according to some, a well-served mission is equivalent to fifty years of normal service in the Church, as a young father or mother you will be as prepared for marriage as you would have been if you were an aged grandmother or grandfather. I am very glad that I learned about interpersonal relationships from my experiences with missionary companions before our children arrived. It has made marriage and family life very enjoyable.

As the second coming of Christ approaches, we tend to worry about how we will fare. Doctrine and Covenants 75:16 promises missionaries, "He who is faithful shall overcome all things, and shall be lifted up at the last day." We shall overcome all things—what a marvelous blessing! Those nagging problems we are still struggling with will eventually be overcome. In addition to being "lifted up" at the Second Coming, the Lord further promises that we will participate with him in those sacred events: "You shall be filled with joy and gladness; and know this, that in the day of judgment you shall be judges of that house, and condemn them" (verse 21). He speaks specifically of those people who have rejected the missionaries' message.

The problem with beginning a chapter like this one is that on almost every page of the scriptures is another promise that the Lord makes to those who are willing to forsake the world and live the gospel. To those who forsake family and loved ones to aid him in saving souls, the Lord says:

> I, the Lord, am merciful and gracious unto those who fear me, and delight to honor those who serve me in righteousness and in truth unto the end.
>
> Great shall be their reward and eternal shall be their glory.
>
> And to them will I reveal all mysteries, yea, all the hidden mysteries of my kingdom from days of old and for ages to come, will I make known unto them the

good pleasure of my will concerning all things pertaining to my kingdom.

Yea, even the wonders of eternity shall they know, and things to come will I show them, even the things of many generations.

And their wisdom shall be great, and their understanding reach to heaven; and before them the wisdom of the wise shall perish, and the understanding of the prudent shall come to naught (D&C 76:5–9).

Missionaries who take the time to ponder the lessons they learned in their missions and who strive to apply those lessons in their lives will realize that they have been enriched in countless ways. When you add the eternal perspective, nothing you can do in time or eternity will bring a higher return on your time investment than a well-served mission. How shortsighted and foolish are those who decide they can't afford to take time out of work or schooling to serve a mission. They will learn, probably too late, how wrong they were. Maybe we can help a few realize their mistake before it is too late.

What a thrilling experience you will have. You have waited for thousands, if not millions, of years for this very hour. Your preparation period, which extends far into the premortal past, is over. "Lift up your heart and rejoice, for the hour of your mission is come" (D&C 31:3). You are earning for yourself and your descendants eternal glory. Now is your time to serve. *Serve with honor!*

INDEX

INDEX